# When the Saints Come Storming In

Other Victor Titles
by Leslie B. Flynn

*Did I Say That?*
*Holy Contradictions*
*19 Gifts of the Spirit*
*The Sustaining Power of Hope*
*The Twelve*
*Your Inner You*

# When the Saints Come Storming In

Formerly titled
*Great Church Fights*
updated and expanded

## Leslie B. Flynn

# VICTOR BOOKS®
A DIVISION OF SCRIPTURE PRESS PUBLICATIONS INC.
USA CANADA ENGLAND

Most Bible quotations are from the *King James Version*. Other quotations are from the *New American Standard Bible* (NASB), © the Lockman Foundation 1960, 1962, 1963, 1968, 1971, 1972, 1973, 1975, 1977; the *Holy Bible, New International Version* (NIV), © 1973, 1978, 1984, International Bible Society. Used by permission of Zondervan Bible Publishers; *Revised Standard Version of the Bible* (RSV), © 1946, 1952, 1971, 1973. Used by permission; and *The New Testament in Modern English, Revised Edition*, (PH), © J.B. Phillips, 1958, 1960, 1972 permission of Macmillan Publishing Co. and Collins Publishers. Used by permission.

Recommended Dewey Decimal Classification: 230:241
Suggested Subject Heading: DOCTRINE; CHRISTIAN CONDUCT

Library of Congress Catalog Card Number: 87-62470

ISBN: 0-89693-471-3

# Contents

*To Iver and Jean Iversen,*
*loyal, gracious people*

# Preface

"Holy Wars" stood out in bold letters on *Newsweek* magazine's cover in the spring of 1987. The cover article reported the lurid adultery-and-hush money scandal that forced TV evangelists Jim and Tammy Bakker to leave the multimillion dollar ministry they founded. The article also told of rivalries among other big-name TV evangelists who hurled acrimonious charges at each other. *Time* magazine also referred to the same matter on its cover the same week, only titling it "Unholy Row." The ruckus, holy or unholy, gave TV evangelism a black eye, and indirectly hurt the whole evangelical movement, as coverage continued during the next weeks on the pages of local and national newspapers, and dominated eleven of Ted Koppel's "Nightline" telecasts.

Almost every week we hear of some ecclesiastical conflict:

— A pastor is dismissed for no real reason.

— Marian Guinn, longtime member of the Church of Christ in Collinsville, Oklahoma, sues the church and its elders for invasion of her privacy because they reprimanded her publicly in a Sunday morning service, and is awarded over $300,000 in actual and punitive damages.

— A church splits down the middle over what hymnbook to use, what color to paint the nursery, or whether or not to relocate.

— The U.S. Justice Department impanels a grand jury to hear allegations of tax fraud against the PTL ministry.

— Members of a church form cliques who will not speak to each other, even at Communion services.

— Well-known evangelist Jack Van Impe actually observes

7

highly regarded pastors fighting publicly over decision cards backstage at the close of a crusade.

— Religious "scandal sheets" include much name-calling, mud-slinging, and muckraking.

— After Oral Roberts makes claim to raising the dead, James Dobson, president of the National Association of Christian Psychotherapists and Counselors, says that such Jesus-like claims show "the need for a serious psychiatric examination. He's killing his ministry" (*Newsweek*, July 13, 1987, p. 52).

Hearing a commotion on his return from work, a father discovered his daughter and playmates in heated quarrel. At his reprimand the little girl innocently explained, "Oh, we're just playing church!"

However, to characterize God's people as wrangling malcontents is to caricature the church. Feuds, factions, fracases, and fusses—yes, the Christian church has had its share, some of them necessary. But let's never forget that fellowship and fervent love have far exceeded the friction.

Let's also remember that the early church, so often idealized and idolized, had its share of dissension. The list of apostolic churches where contention broke out reads like an ecclesiastical hall of fame: Jerusalem, Antioch, Corinth, Rome, Phillipi, Thessalonica, and by implication, several others.

No church today can escape dissension completely. Where there's vitality, differences of opinion are likely to develop. The real question is: Will disagreements divide and wound the Christian body, or will these controversies draw the members together in deepened understanding and commitment?

This book does not pretend to enumerate all causes of church strife, nor catalog all known remedies. Rather, it surveys most of the major New Testament episodes of contention, plus the measures taken to resolve them, in the hope that biblical insights and principles will help twentieth-century churches to turn their internal skirmishes into training grounds for victory. Friction wisely resolved can move the church ahead for God's glory.

Conflict is certain. Conflict can be destructive or constructive. It's how we handle conflict that counts.

# 1.

## We Need Each Other

I was mugged tonight!

Looking for an address on my usual Tuesday night visitation I was directed under a tunnel and up to the second floor landing of an apartment complex in a town thirty miles from New York City by two young men. Just as I realized this was not the right place, one of them jumped me. "This is a stickup. Give me your wallet or I'll kill you." Quickly I surrendered my wallet. He passed it to his accomplice. Spotting my ungloved hand, he said, "You have a ring."

With the release of his arm, up to now pressed tightly against my nose, mouth, and throat, I was able to speak. I said, "I am a preacher." At this he backed off and walked down to the first floor. Anxious for fresh air, I followed. Outside, he handed me back my wallet, already stripped of all money but thankfully still containing all my credit cards and other important items.

Returning to my church, I had a few thoughts. One was never to go back to that area after dark. Another, facetiously, was to ask the board of trustees to put money in the budget for pistol practice and for serving in a hazardous occupation. I also resolved never to fly the Concord, for that speedy oceanic flight would permit me to be mugged in both London and New

York on the same day. I also asked the Lord not to be so graphic in answering my prayers for gripping sermonic illustrations—I had just announced a pre-Easter sermon series on Jesus and the two thieves.

Later that evening, working on this chapter, I thought of the fact that sometimes Christians are guilty of mugging each other—maybe not physically, but in the manner Paul meant when he warned believers against biting and devouring one another (Gal. 5:15). In fact my local paper that very night reported on a continuing church dispute in another town five miles away. Front-page headlines on previous days read like this:

"Church Locked, Chained. Trustees Shut Church. Deacons Will Try to Reopen It."

A few days later: "Ousted Pastor Holds Sidewalk Service."

Days later: "Deacon Cuts Chains Locking Church Door."

Again: "Church Re-chained from Inside."

That very day's headline: "Members Battle over Control of Church. Judge Puts Minister's Fate in Congregation's Hands."

As this is written, the case has not been settled, but regardless of the outcome, everyone will be a loser, the church will long be the laughingstock of the community, and the name of Christ will have been dragged in the mud.

A rather telling picture appeared on the front page of our paper when this story first broke. It was a real-life photo of this troubled church, cut in half and separated down the middle by a narrow, jagged band of space containing the word "divided." The photo reminded me of a cartoon showing two sections of a congregation, sitting with backs to each other and each facing a side wall, with the preacher intoning, "It's come to my attention that there's been a split in the church."

Though most church conflicts never make the daily newspaper, almost every congregation experiences some dissension at one time or other. Through the centuries the church of Jesus Christ, instead of majoring in communion, has often muddled in contention. Despite the halo of spirituality imagined over the apostolic church, the dust clouds of sharp collisions were equally visible. As long as Christians care about the church, and as long as they cannot completely divest themselves of their old nature, they will be unable to achieve perfect unity, and will disagree on certain matters.

If all denominations could be abolished, within a decade or two we would probably have most of the same varieties again, perhaps with different names, but emphasizing distinctives deemed important. The Pentecostals would still be lifting hands in worship, and Baptists would still be starting competing churches in the same town—First, Second, Third, etc.!

Every congregation these days includes the traditionalist and the innovator. Tension will pulsate between those who want to maintain the status quo and those who wish to branch into something new. Some yearn for quiet hymns; others demand songs with ear-splitting volume. Some enjoy a fixed order of service; others prefer it unstructured. Some revel in reverent dignity; others respond to enthusiastic handclapping. Said one pastor, "If my people decided to evangelize our town, some would advocate tract distribution with door-to-door visitation, while others would bring in church-growth experts."

Distressing are the differences which stem from ulterior motives or personality conflicts. Some exploit fellow members for personal prestige, business purposes, or financial profit. How grievous to see headlines which read, "Ex-Aide Sues Evangelist," or "Church Treasurer Indicted." Some men, dominated by a boss at work or by a wife at home, throw their weight around at church. A middle-aged member strode out of church enraged at the songleader because he had omitted the third verse of the four-verse closing hymn. The real reason for his excessive outburst—his strong, longtime personal dislike of the songleader.

All confrontations are not necessarily evil. Marriage counselors point out that, though conflict is inevitable in the marriage relationship, a dispute need not be a destructive force. An argument joined with the right attitude can clarify issues, promote a better understanding of viewpoints, and fuse a decision good for both.

13

Similarly, all conflict in ecclesiastical life is not unhealthy per se. Disagreements with their accompanying misunderstanding, hurt feelings, and competitiveness do carry the potential of destructive bitterness, but if they are properly handled through peaceable, God-given wisdom, they can be a constructive force for uniting the body of Christ (James 3:13-18).

## We Are The Family of God

Two porcupines in northern Canada huddled together to get warm, according to a forest folktale. But their quills pricked each other, so they moved apart. Before long they were shivering, so they sidled close again. Soon both were getting jabbed again. Same story; same ending. They needed each other, but they kept needling each other.

Though through the centuries the saints have needled each other, we do need each other, for we are members of the family of God. Believers are knit together in an invisible yet intimate relationship. The Apostles' Creed calls it the "communion of saints." A mission board doctrinal statement phrases it, "We believe in the spiritual unity of believers in Christ." Paul tells us, "For ye are all the children of God by faith in Christ Jesus" (Gal. 3:26).

Two of Jesus' disciples came from diametrically opposite backgrounds. Matthew, a tax collector for the Roman government, engaged in an occupation considered traitorous by Jewish patriots. Simon, a recent member of the Zealot party with its nationalistic passion, must have found it difficult to accept a former collaborationist such as Matthew. But Jesus prayed that they—and the other apostles as well—would all be one (John 17:11). Through Jesus' redemptive work, not only tax-collector Matthew and zealot Simon, but all believers of all ages and places regardless of background have been united in one Spirit. Accordingly, Paul spoke of the universal Christian church as one body with Christ as Head, and believers as harmoniously functioning members.

Genuine unity does not come through organization. Tying two chickens together and hanging them over a clothesline may give some semblance of union, but definitely not unity. Organizational unity of church denominations is secondary to the spiritual unity of true Christians. The National Association of Evangelicals lists 38 complete denominations, plus individual churches from other groups, among its 36,000 member churches, all confessing a common faith. Christians of numerous denominations attending a Billy Graham rally sense a oneness with other believers, despite their varying forms of government and doctrinal emphases; some Fundamentalists would, however, not be included. Those in attendance sing with deep significance:

> We are not divided,
> All one body we,
> One in hope and doctrine,
> One in charity.

True spiritual kinship transcends not only organizational but natural relationships as well. Two brothers, one a Christian and the other a member of a fraternal organization, were touring Europe. One day they encountered a missionary from America. Immediately the Christian brother and the missionary began an animated conversation on spiritual matters.

Later the club-loving brother remarked, "I didn't know you knew that missionary. Where did you meet him?" The Christian replied that he had never seen the missionary before, whereupon his brother exclaimed, "You talked like long-lost friends."

Replied the brother, "That's exactly how we felt, because we belong to the same Lord."

The second most frequently used name in the New Testament for a Christian is "brother." Since God has appointed believers to be conformed to the image of His Son so "that He might be the firstborn among many brethren" (Rom. 8:29), then all children of God are brothers or sisters of Jesus Christ, and of each other. How can we become unbrotherly to someone who is our brother?

Perhaps the most graphic use of this title was Ananias' greeting to "Brother Saul," the newly converted persecutor of Christians who had come to Damascus to imprison followers of "the way" (Acts 9:17). The great apostle never forgot that greeting, mentioning it a quarter century later while relating his conversion story to the Sanhedrin (22:13). When we recall that later the apostles at Jerusalem at first doubted Paul's sincerity, this warm greeting, showing immediate filial acceptance by Ananias, is all the more remarkable (9:26). Perhaps a more generous use of "brother" or "sister" in Christian salutations today would remind us that we should be exercising family love in our fellowships.

If you identify your closest friends, isn't it true that you came to know each other because each of you first came to know Christ? He is the common bond that knits all believers together, enabling us to sing with genuine fervor, "Blest be the tie that binds our hearts in Christian love."

## Every Family Has Fights

A motorist asked a boy how to find a certain church. The boy thought for a moment and gave these directions: "Go one block south and you'll see a church on the corner. That's the United Church. Go one block more, and you'll come on a church that's not united. That's it!"

One Sunday years ago TV viewers who tuned into a morning service of the First Baptist Church of Atlanta were shocked when a man stepped up to the new pastor, Charles Stanley, and took a swing at him. The church had been searching for a new pastor and had finally promoted young Charles Stanley from an assistant position to senior pastor. The man who attacked him had strongly objected to his appointment. The promotion, however, obviously was in God's plan if not in the plan of the pugnacious church member. Dr. Stanley's powerful preaching has touched the lives of thousands in the thriving Atlanta church and through TV and radio outreach.

Churches everywhere become disunited. Though we need each other, sometimes we needle—or mug—each other. Even

Paul, strong advocate of unity that he was, found himself embroiled in personal and ecclesiastical disputes. The "church fights" related in the New Testament frankly acknowledge the foibles of early saints which coexisted along with their good qualities.

The young church's first recorded conflict concerned the complaint of Grecians against Hebrews because their widows were neglected in the daily food apportionment (Acts 6:1-6).

Paul publicly rebuked Peter for open prejudice against Gentile believers (Gal. 2:11-14).

Those with strong convictions about circumcision criticized Peter for bringing the Gospel to Gentiles (Acts 11:2-3). The same reason caused "no small dissension and disputation" between Paul and the circumcision party who believed this rite essential to salvation (15:1-2). This simmering controversy precipitated the first church council and "much debate" among its leaders (v. 7, NASB).

A sharp disagreement between Paul and Barnabas over whether to take Mark on a second missionary journey caused them to break up and go their separate ways (15:36-40).

The Corinthian church verged on a split with at least four factions campaigning for different leaders (1 Cor. 1:11-12). This division widened when spiritual brothers went to court against each other (6:1-11), and the well-to-do declined to share their food with the poor at church "love-feasts" (11:18-23).

Two factions developed at Rome over the eating of meat associated with sacrifice to idols, and over the observance of holy days (Rom. 14:1-6).

A disagreement between two prominent women of the Philippian church, Euodias and Syntyche, brought a written appeal from Paul for reconciliation (Phil. 4:2-3). Because Jesus had expected such disputes He had earlier given instructions for both offending and offended parties (Matt. 5:23-24; 18:15-17).

Hints of strife among early saints crop up many times. Paul exhorted the Philippians to "do everything without complaining

**17**

or arguing" (Phil. 2:14). James implied the presence of battles among the brethren when he asked the source of "wars and fightings among you" (James 4:1). He traced this to selfish ambition and bitter jealousy in their hearts (James 3:14).

A lust for preeminence prompted Diotrophes to expel fellow brethren from the church (3 John 9-10).

Somebody wrote:

> To dwell above with saints we love,
> That will be grace and glory.
> To live below with saints we know,
> That's another story!

## Keeping Peace in the Family

Relatives have good reasons for strong relationships. Brothers who are unbrotherly are a contradiction. A church family should be warm and mutually supporting. Though believers cannot always get along smoothly with fellow believers, neither can they get along without each other. A glowing coal removed from others in the fireplace will soon lose its warmth and light. A member of a nonloving church said, "Our church has real unity. We're frozen together."

For believers to function in friction is much like a car running without lubrication. For believers to bitterly separate from other genuine Christians and speak of "them" as opposed to "we" is as incongruous as for a hand to consider itself independent from the heart that pumps it blood. We must beware of promoting a "many-bodies-of-Christ" stance. Rather, believers are one body, and all belong to each other.

The Spirit does not want schism, but solidarity in Christ's body. The eye has need of the ear, as does the hand of the foot. Competition cleaves the body, but care coordinates it. When each member of the body functions harmoniously with all the other members of the body, the result is health and strength.

In a *Peanuts* cartoon Lucy demanded that Linus change TV channels, threatening him with her fist if he didn't.

WE NEED EACH OTHER

"What makes you think you can walk right in here and take over?" asks Linus.

"These five fingers," says Lucy. "Individually they're nothing but when I curl them together like this into a single unit, they form a weapon that is terrible to behold."

"Which channel do you want?" asks Linus.

Turning away, he looks at his fingers and says, "Why can't you guys get organized like that?"

One of the great side effects of Billy Graham crusades is the way in which the common objective of evangelism brings Christians and churches together. Time and time again believers comment, "I wish we'd learned to work together like this years ago!" Their experience resembles that of two sailors fighting fiercely on the upper deck of a ship; suddenly they heard another sailor shout, "Man overboard!" Without a moment's hesitation, both fighting men plunged into the sea to rescue the drowning man. When they surfaced, both were helping the man in distress. Working together makes for peace.

Unity validates the Gospel. Jesus declared, "By this shall all men know that ye are My disciples, if ye have love one to another" (John 13:35). On the other hand, disunity disgraces the cause of Christ. How ironic that last year's *Time* cover article titled, "TV's Unholy Row," describing rivalries and acrimonious remarks among TV preachers, and captioned, "A sex-and-money scandal tarnishes electronic evangelism," began with a New Testament quote, "Lead a life worthy of the calling to which you have been called, with all lowliness and meekness, with patience, forbearing one another in love, eager to maintain the unity of the Spirit in the bond of peace" (Eph. 4:1-3).

The Apostle Paul, who wrote these words, gave high priority to the maintaining of unity. He recognized that since the unity of the Spirit was already a reality in Christ, we do not need to originate it, but rather to strive to keep it. Thus, over and over Paul encourages the pursuit of peace. "Live in harmony with one another" (Rom. 12:16, NIV). "If it is possible, as far as it depends on you, live at peace with everyone" (v. 18, NIV). "Let us therefore follow after the things which make for peace" (Rom. 14:19). "Be at peace among yourselves" (1 Thes. 5:13).

Leaders have a vital role in peacekeeping, therefore their character should be free of belligerence, violence, quarrelsomeness, and impetuousness (1 Tim. 3:3; Titus 1:7). The Lord's servant must be kind to everyone (2 Tim. 2:24).

Paul does not push "peace at any price." Scandal, factional schism, and distortion of basic doctrine require disciplinary action, because purity in faith and conduct is essential to unity. Sometimes disfellowshipping the unrepentant party, such as at Corinth, is necessary for the peace and strength of the body members (1 Cor. 5:1-5).

God is called "the God of peace" several times in the Bible (Rom. 16:20; 1 Thes. 5:23; 2 Thes. 3:16; Heb. 13:20). To the division-torn church at Corinth Paul writes, "God is not a God of confusion, but of peace" (1 Cor. 14:33, NASB). The ultimate healer of all church rifts is the God of peace.

An American doctor traveling in Korea knew just enough of the language to get around. At a station stop an elderly Korean boarded the train and sat across from the doctor. He carried a large bundle in a white cloth. Soon the Korean began to speak to the doctor, pouring out a torrent of words. The doctor replied with the only sentence he had memorized, "I do not understand Korean." The old man persisted. A second time the doctor gave his stock answer. This was repeated a third time.

In the stream of Korean words, the doctor thought he had detected a somewhat familiar word. Had the old man said something about Jesus? His doubt vanished when the Korean pointed to the doctor and asked, "Yesu? Yesu?" With a smile the doctor nodded agreement, "Yesu, Yesu."

Smiling from ear to ear, the Korean opened his large bundle and proudly displayed his Korean Bible. Then he put his finger on a verse. The doctor couldn't read it, of course, but carefully figuring out the approximate place in his own Bible, he read

1 John 3:14, "We know that we have passed out of death into life, because we love the brethren" (NASB).

The barriers of language, culture, and age fell as the unity of the Holy Spirit flowed between the two men. The Korean turned to another text, this one found in almost the exact center of the Bible, which the doctor was also able to locate: "Behold, how good and how pleasant it is for brethren to dwell together in unity!" (Ps. 133:1) As the train rolled along, the two believers rejoiced in warm Christian fellowship.

If two saints with such contrasting backgrounds can experience the unity of the Spirit, can not we who fellowship in the same church circles overcome lesser obstacles to enrich each other and glorify God?

The Puritan Thomas Brookes penned, "For wolves to worry the lambs is no wonder, but for one lamb to worry another, this is unnatural and monstrous" (I.D.E. Thomas, *Puritan Quotations*, Moody Press, p. 304).

No one relishes family life that reverberates with tension and feuding. Our spiritual health and fruitfulness require that we "keep the peace, brother."

# 2.
# *Early Friction*

When the World Evangelical Fellowship (WEF) with its fifty-six fellowships met in its general assembly in England in 1980, two of the delegations were deeply disturbed by WEF's invitation to two Roman Catholic observers to attend the sessions. The Italian Evangelical Alliance withdrew from the world association, while the Spanish Evangelical Alliance put its membership into abeyance. Their actions protested WEF's tendency to relate to Roman Catholicism in an uncritical way.

The WEF Theological Commission responded by creating an Ecumenical Issues Task Force with the assignment of formulating a consensus position on the relationships of evangelicals to Roman Catholic doctrine and practice. Their report, produced after two years of work, noted favorable trends in Roman Catholicism but also obstacles seriously impeding fellowship with evangelicals. This major statement was adopted at WEF's general assembly in Singapore in June 1986 involving 250 representatives from 61 countries.

Representatives from Italy and Spain were especially appreciative of the statement. A few months later, in October, the Italian Evangelical Association unanimously passed a resolution authorizing a return to the WEF fold.

A major factor in the reconciliation process was the strong

representation given the two unhappy countries. With three members each appointed from Italy and Spain, a total of six out of a committee of seventeen (over a third), the task force was weighted to provide adequate attention to their grievances.

This episode recalls the first recorded dissension in the early church where, to settle it, the majority of referees were appointed from the group with the grievance. It was as if to say, "You who are dissatisfied, we need your input; here's the authority to do whatever is necessary to rectify the injustice and set things right."

Easily we forget that the early church had discord. Often someone laments, "If only we could return to the good old days of the apostolic church." Yes, from the vantage point of distance it does shine brightly. We recall the believers at Jerusalem faithfully observing doctrine, fellowship, the breaking of bread, and prayer. Somehow we extend this glowing picture into a fantasy of perfection, a church without problems. But the realistic biblical account tells how the unity was shattered by internal complaint.

## The Paradox of Conflict

Conflict is simply a clash of differing points of view, of opinions, of values. Discord among the believers in those early months seems so contradictory.

● *The church was prospering numerically.* The first rift broke out "while the disciples were increasing in number" (Acts 6:1, NASB). Affluence can be dangerous to churches as well as to individuals, bringing complacency and false confidence. More people may mean more trouble; prosperity may produce problems. So it was here. Success created a potentially serious situation.

● *The church basked in the afterglow of Pentecost.* Only a few months before, at Pentecost, the disciples were filled with the Holy Spirit. Three thousand were converted to Christ. By now the number had expanded to about 5,000 (Acts 4:4). Jews of both Palestinian and foreign backgrounds had been molded into loving unity. But the oneness of the groups with differing cultures was threatening to come apart. However, the Pentecostal glow still lingered.

● *The church shared all things in common.* From the beginning, through the prompting of the Holy Spirit, believers pooled their resources and shared with needy brothers. This beautiful spirit of community not only displayed the remarkable fruit of their love in Christ, but demonstrated that money given to alleviate poverty is just as spiritual as funds designated for missions.

The record reads, "The multitude of them that believed were of one heart and of one soul: neither said any of them that ought of the things which he possessed was his own; but they had all things common (Acts 4:32). According to *Clarke's Commentary,* some manuscripts add, "And there was no kind of difference or dissension among them."

● *Pinnacle of piety.* It was at this summit of harmony that Satan tried to undermine with a two-pronged attack. First, he tempted Ananias and Sapphira to pretend to emulate the example of the others who sold property and gave the money to the church. This couple withheld some of the sale price, while acting as though they had contributed every bit of the proceeds. Their hypocrisy was exposed and drastically judged by the Holy Spirit through Peter.

Second, Satan tried to gain a foothold at the point of sacrificial sharing by stirring up dissension over the uneven distribution of this charity. So the glimmering bubble of a perfect church burst with this first case of in-church feuding.

● *Conflict not a "no-no."* The imperfection of even regenerate human nature makes some conflict inevitable. In any organization, ecclesiastical or secular, leadership creates a certain tension, declares Richard Wolff in *Man at the Top.* "Not every conflict is necessarily neurotic. Some is normal and healthy. The tension between what is and what ought to be—the gap between reality and ideal—is indispensable to well-being. Every challenge carries tension within itself. We do not need a tensionless state, but a challenging goal and purpose" (Tyndale, 1969, p. 77).

## When the Saints Come Storming In

In their book *Church Fights,* Speed Leas and Paul Kittlaus suggest that any church without problems "would be a very dumb, shallow, and depressing kind of place." They deplore the fact that conflict is a feared "no-no," that it always produces guilt feelings. On the contrary, they suggest, church people "can handle conflict and, in fact, enjoy challenging and being challenged." Churches do exist that have a history of dealing with conflicts, both large and small, "fairly and openly, and where the membership is not immobilized by a difference of opinion" (Westminster Press, 1973, p. 72).

Such was the case in the church's first recorded dispute. It faced the problem squarely and charitably, so that out of trouble came triumph.

● *A murmuring.* Luke, the writer of Acts, states the situation, "When the number of disciples was increasing, the Grecian Jews among them complained against the Hebraic Jews because their widows were being overlooked in the daily distribution of food" (6:1, NIV).

Two groups were mentioned, though both were Jews. Both worshiped Jehovah; both were loyal to Christ; both were of the same nation and blood; but their customs were different. The Greek-speaking Hebrew Christians had come under the influence of Greek culture when they or their ancestors lived outside Israel. Though the Holy City had a majority of Aramaic-speaking Hebrews, a large number of Grecian Jews lived there. "There were dwelling at Jerusalem Jews, devout men, out of every nation under heaven" (Acts 2:5). At least fifteen of those nations are mentioned (2:8-11).

Both groups included widows in need of material help. In the early weeks, no one lacked because possessors of lands and houses sold them and brought the proceeds to the apostles to share with the needy. But now came this strong complaint to complicate their harmony.

Was the grievance justified? Likely it was. The word *neglected,* used only here in the New Testament, means literally "to look beyond, to view amiss, overlook, slight." The imperfect tense of the verb indicates continuous action, hinting that the

26

neglect had gone on for some time.

Was the slight intentional? Perhaps some prejudice did flare. Just as today's Sabras (Israel-born Jews) subconsciously consider themselves superior to foreign-born Jews, so Hebrews of the first century often regarded Grecian Jews as second-class citizens. Maybe the Hebrew element, in the majority and in charge, regarded their Hellenistic brethren as having only a secondary claim on their food. After all—this was Jerusalem, and these people were foreigners. So if the funds were short, the Grecians may have been assigned a smaller share.

But it seems more likely the neglect was accidental. If the brethren loved others enough to sell possessions to meet their needs, wouldn't they likely also show impartiality in the distribution of the proceeds? Besides, James, a strong influence in the Jerusalem church, strongly advocated helping "widows in their affliction" (James 1:27). As the church grew in numbers and in need, the logistics of distribution became too complex for the apostles who apparently had jurisdiction over the matter (Acts 4:35). In any case, the Grecian widows were slighted. Who would speak up for them? The community's peace was jeopardized. Action had to be taken.

Incidentally, the sharing of assets by a community has had a poor track record through the centuries. Even in this case, before many years, Barnabas (and Paul later) had to gather offerings to alleviate the poverty at Jerusalem and in surrounding Judea (11:27-30).

## Facing the Problem

A healthy group requires open expression of feelings, not repression. Avoiding problems multiplies problems, such as the lingering agony of unresolved tension, the playing of clever games, and the sapping of energies used in side-stepping the issue which could have been used toward a solution.

Leas and Kittlaus say: "Where groups tend to suppress conflict, there will be an accumulation of feeling, leading toward a potentially dangerous conflict. A group in conflict can be like a pressure cooker. As the heat (conflict) increases, the pressure builds up. The more pressure, the greater the explosion if the pressure is not abated. . . . Pressure can build up, causing a large explosion over a rather minor conflict. . . . For example, we encountered a conflict where a minister lost his church over the question whether the memorial plaque for the church's members who have died would be in the narthex or in the social hall" (*Church Fights*, pp. 47–48). Hostile feelings can be re-directed toward a safe target.

In *Leadership*, Ronald Kraybill, director of the Mennonite Conciliation Service in Akron, Pennsylvania, tells of visiting on successive weekends two churches facing the same issue of disagreement. The first church seemed to hush the subject up with people withdrawing from each other when the discussion did occur. The second church didn't try to hide its differences but encouraged a vigorous exchange of ideas. Observed Kraybill, "It's odd, but this church, which wasn't trying to bury its conflict, actually seemed to have less of it" (*Fall Quarter*, 1986, p. 32).

● *Don't gloss over.* Kraybill suggests four ways people who fear conflict commonly respond to disagreements: spiritualizing, denying, trivializing, and guilt-tripping. Here are hypothetical reactions of early saints to the alms-distribution controversy that illustrate these four categories:

*Spiritualizing*—"What we really need is not discussion, but prayer. We should get down on our knees, confess our sins, and that'll take care of our problems."

*Denying*—"I don't see any problem. I get along with everyone here. Why does everybody keep fussing? There's really no trouble."

*Trivializing*—"We shouldn't be bothered by so trifling a matter as food. Here we sit surrounded by a sea of lost souls. We shouldn't be concerned about the meat that perishes. Shouldn't we rather concentrate on the meat which endures to eternal life?"

*Guilt-tripping*—"We're not doing a very good job," the twelve apostles may have confided among themselves. "Perhaps we're not providing good leadership."

Instead, the apostles accepted the situation, including any indirect criticism for failure in alms distribution, and set about to right the situation. They admitted a fire was smoldering and hurried to extinguish it before it became a conflagration of defiling bitterness. They wisely suffered the short-lived pain of coping with the grievance. They reasoned that problems should be brought up, not bottled up.

The apostles sensed an additional danger in the situation. The archenemy of the church was taking double aim at the infant fellowship, not only creating dissension, but trying to sidetrack the Twelve from their main ministry. The apostles had been called to prayer and the ministry of God's Word, but along the way they had been responsible for the ministry of distributing alms to the needy. Now tempted to devote more time to this charitable service, they realized they would be diverted from their primary calling. So with divine insight, they resisted the temptation, asserting it would be a serious mistake for them to neglect the Word of God to wait on tables (Acts 6:2). They would get help.

By delegating this task to others, they were not suggesting that alms distribution was any less sacred than prayer and preaching. One ministered the living Bread, the other material bread; one by speaking, the other by supervising. They knew that the harmonious working of a church depended on wise apportionment of its functions, just as the physical body operates smoothly when each of its parts performs its God-given task.

## Involving the Congregation

Regardless of a church's form of government, it is wise to involve the entire membership in certain church-wide matters. The apostles, after some preliminary thinking on the problem, convened the community of believers, inviting the help of all. To the assembled disciples, the apostles proposed their plan, then said, "Select from among you, brethren, seven men . . . whom we may put in charge of this task" (6:3, NASB).

Though the apostles suggested the solution, the entire congregation accepted the plan (6:5). The verse also notes that the congregation chose seven helpers, then presented them to the apostles. Here democracy, not clerical dictatorship, was part of the solution.

At the suggestion of the apostles, seven servants, or deacons, were chosen. Why seven? Many answers have been suggested. Because every Jewish village or town was presided over by seven leaders. Or because there were seven days in the week, one day for each deacon. Or because there were perhaps seven churches or districts, in Jerusalem, with each having one representative. Or because the number of converts now approached 7,000. Or because seven is a frequent and favorite biblical number!

Though the number seven is not a pattern to be necessarily followed in present-day church government, nor are these servants the equivalent of the deacons mentioned in Timothy, their qualifications are worthy of emulation. They were chosen not because they were somebody's relative or friend, or were successful or rich or personable, but because they measured up to a four-fold criterion of fitness. The apostles asked the congregation to select men who were:

(1) believers—"among you,"
(2) reputable—"of good reputation,"
(3) Spirit-controlled—"full of the Spirit,"
(4) wise—"full . . . of wisdom" (6:3, NASB).

The humble duties of table-serving amazingly called for sterling Christian graces plus sanctified common sense, enabling these deacons to administer tactfully and lovingly in this delicate situation.

## Agreeing on Procedure

Ronald Kraybill in the same *Leadership* article tells of a "holy war" he mediated. Toward the end of a quiet semiannual business meeting, someone noted that the music committee had asked for a 20 percent increase in budget. When asked why, the chairman of the music committee explained that the two part-time staff people were overworked, and thus the committee had decided to hire a part-time director for the junior choir. Immediately two members jumped to their feet in objection. People in the pews stiffened. A few slipped out the back door.

A member of the music committee angrily defended the proposal, accusing members of the congregation of exploiting the gifts of musicians and trying to sabotage the finest church music program in town. In essence, this explosion was the result of a long-smoldering fuse. Each year the music committee asked for more budget, and every year others opposed the hiring of music staff. Would they go on to a higher music budget, or hold the line?

The chairman, caught off guard, wisely summarized the differing viewpoints and suggested lodging the issue with the church council to take leadership in resolving the disagreement. The council formed a committee representing the various views and set up a proposed process, commonly called in mediation circles the "Agreement." Submitted to the congregation for approval before any council discussion, the Agreement contained four items: issue, goals, time line, and decision rule.

The real *issue* proved to be voluntary versus paid service in the music ministry, not whether to increase the music budget.

*Goals* involved the open, tolerant discussion of the issue with opportunity for all members to express their views and to reach a proposal hopefully acceptable to a maximum number of the congregation.

*Time line* provided a schedule with ample time for all groups to meet and reach a final proposal.

*Decision rule* specified a 66 percent affirmative vote by the congregation on any resolution recommended by the church council ad hoc committee.

Upshot of the whole process was to maintain the status quo in regard to paid music service.

Mediation facilitators strongly emphasize the encouragement of group dialogue, using a variety of methods to structure people participation.

## Going the Second Mile

A significant factor in the solution of the early-church friction is indicated by the names of the deacons chosen. All seven bear Hellenistic names. Though some Hebrew Jews did have Greek names, the likelihood is that these men were all deliberately selected from the Hellenistic group.

The Hebrew majority could have officiously insisted, "We won't let those Greeks put anything over on us. We deserve a larger representation and the authority to see that things are done right." But here was a generous act of peacemaking by which the Hebrews said, "You think your widows are being neglected. Then choose Grecian men to distribute the daily food. We're trusting the entire operation to you."

This policy has been followed outside church affairs. William Penn insisted in his colony that court cases involving Indians would have red men make up at least half of the jury.

Many churches have adopted conciliatory measures when a minority was grieved. In one disagreement between church youth and the decision-making adults over the time and rooms for a summer youth program, the official board appointed a committee with more young members than adults to work out the matter. The grateful youth responded with unexpected consideration for the adults.

In a church vote the group who wins by a minimal amount should not lord it over the losing side, but rather should consider a second vote after a few weeks of prayer and meditation. A church in the East acting on a motion to adopt a relocation program voted 51 percent in favor and 49 percent against. Applause broke out among the 51 percent. The drama had all the potential for a church split. Someone on the winning side stood, "We do not have the mind of the Lord. I move that we rescind the action." The vote to rescind was unanimous. The church took thirty days for prayer. The next vote was 88 percent to relocate. When the 12 percent saw how God had changed others, they began to rethink their decision. By the end of the evening, the vote was practically unanimous.

The "soft" answer by the Hebrew element turned away the

incipient wrath of the Hellenists. Their action said, "We need each other. We'll bear each other's burdens." Love overcame. Hebrew and Greek bowed their heads as the apostles led in prayer and laid hands of dedication on the seven deacons. The fellowship's first serious friction was beautifully mended and ended.

## Capitalizing on Crisis

Dissension need not bring disaster, but may bring delightful dividends as in this case.

• *Numerical increase.* Satan was unable to wedge in and split this church. The congregation's extremity became God's opportunity. As outsiders observed this fusion of fellowship, they were convinced of the reality of Christ. Had not Jesus said, "By this shall all men know that ye are My disciples, if ye have love one to another"? (John 13:35) Wearing the badge of love led to a harvest of souls. "And the word of God increased, and the number of disciples multiplied in Jerusalem greatly" (Acts 6:7).

• *Many priests believed.* Another result was that "a great company of the priests were obedient to the faith" (6:7). As far back as the birth of John the Baptist, priests had heard that Zacharias' son would be the forerunner of the Messiah. In the last three years, priests had heard of Jesus' miracles, especially those to whom cleansed lepers had come to offer a sacrifice after healing by the Galilean. Very recently the priests on duty when Jesus died recounted the ripping of the thick temple curtain from top to bottom, a feat no human hand could have performed. For many convinced of Jesus' messiahship, the final straw to draw them into the fold of faith was observing the love of believers in action.

• *Expansion of the missionary enterprise.* The rest of the Book of Acts with all its Gospel preaching flowed out of this first quarrel, righteously resolved. It happened this way.

Out of complaint came the election of seven deacons. One of the deacons was Stephen. Next verse in sequence (6:8) says, "Stephen, full of faith and power, did great wonders and miracles among the people." Later, Stephen, whose wisdom the Sanhedrin could not answer, was stoned to death.

Out of Stephen's martyrdom came the scattering of the Jerusalem saints throughout Judea and Samaria. Also, Stephen's Christlike death helped goad Paul into surrender to Christ on the Damascus Road.

Out of Paul's conversion and commissioning came his three missionary journeys and the carrying of the Gospel through Asia Minor and Greece, and right to the capital city of Rome.

● *First Church Council.* Oddly, this expansion of the Gospel to the Gentile world precipitated a controversy so serious it led to a major confrontation known as the First Church Council.

Though not all conflicts lead to happy endings, throughout church history disagreement has proven to be the arena in which the church has come to a clearer understanding of God's already revealed truth. Out of the First Church Council came an unequivocal decree of a salvation by pure grace alone, apart from works or ceremony. Many of our church creeds with their statements of orthodoxy have issued from conflict. Witness the Athanasian Creed in its opposition to Arianism.

This same problem of friction between two culturally divergent groups in the same church has been repeated time and time again through the centuries. I am looking right now at a letter dated March 1987 from a South American missionary who asks prayer for a serious dislocation in a church between a group with an Indian background and another with a mainstream Argentine cultural orientation.

Robert Coote, writing in *Evangelical Newsletter* (Sept. 26, 1975) about the problem of racially integrated churches, describes several models, and comments that it's not easy to get to the heart of racism with a real cure. Then he points to an actual documented illustration that might help:

Some years ago a minority group within a Christian community felt cheated. The problem involved the equitable distribution of resources and the treating of the minority with respect and affirmation. The solution would determine whether the minority would be made to feel part of the group, and thus feel truly integrated.

The leaders of the majority came up with a plan. Several responsible men from the minority party were selected, and the money and resources were put in their hands. Henceforth the indigenous leaders of the minority handled the financial responsibility for the entire group, majority and minority alike.

One of the seven became the first Christian martyr in that city. Another became the first Christian evangelist. The beautiful, direct, and simple solution in which they figured is documented in Acts 6.

# 3.

# *Heavyweight Bout*

Evangelist Jack Van Impe was closing a citywide crusade in Green Bay, Wisconsin on a Sunday afternoon in an arena which featured wrestling Sunday nights. On Monday night Rex Humbard was scheduled to begin a series of meetings. The marquee outside the arena read,

JACK VAN IMPE
WRESTLING
REX HUMBARD

Though these widely known men do not maintain a pugnacious relationship, from time to time other prominent Christian leaders have squared off at each other in an unfriendly skirmish.

Tony Campolo, one of the most popular and gifted communicators on the evangelical circuit today, was canceled as a speaker at a national convention called Youth Congress '85. Some of the Congress organizers questioned certain statements in one of his books, even accusing him of heresy. The decision to cancel was made by Bill Bright, president of Campus Crusade for Christ, one of the event's sponsoring organizations.

In an attempt to resolve the situation which Campolo claimed treated him unfairly, he and Bright appeared before a four-member panel convened by the Christian Legal Society, consisting of J.I. Packer, who served as chairman; Gordon MacDonald, then president of Inter-Varsity Christian Fellowship; Earl Radmacher, president of Western Conservative Baptist Seminary; and James Boice, pastor of Tenth Presbyterian Church in Philadelphia.

At a one-day meeting in Chicago, the panel questioned Campolo for a total of six hours, asking him to explain parts of his book, *A Reasonable Faith* (Word), which Bright had cited as the basis for Campolo's cancellation. Bright emphasized that he did not view himself as an adversary of Campolo, stating that the differences were theological, not personal, and affirming him as a "man to whom God has given extraordinary gifts."

In their verdict the panel determined that Campolo could not rightly be called a heretic, but that with some clarification of his book, all accusations of heresy could be withdrawn, and his ministry as a brilliant communicator could then continue with full fruitfulness.

Sam Ericsson, executive director of the Christian Legal Society, said that the meeting "was one of the most intense sessions I've ever witnessed. . . . It was a powerful illustration of the Holy Spirit being very active because Christians decided to do it biblically."

In the early church a strong difference developed between the two outstanding leaders, Peter and Paul. Though no Christian Legal Society existed in those days, the bout between these strong personalities seems to have been quickly settled.

Incidentally, this was the first of three flare-ups to occur in the same city in a few brief years. What would you think of a church that struggled through three serious fights in so short a span? Did these clashes cripple the testimony of that church to the community and world?

The vibrant church at Antioch was the scene of these three major disagreements. Here the warm-hearted Barnabas and the logically minded Paul taught for a year; here irrepressible believers were first called Christians; here relief funds were collected for the famine-stricken saints in Jerusalem and Judea; and here the first missionaries to the Gentile world were commissioned.

The altercation between Peter and Paul (this chapter) was the first. The second (chapter 4) was the acute dissension over the question of faith plus circumcision that led to the first Jerusalem Council (Acts 14:26-28; 15:1-2). The third (chapter 5) was the sharp controversy that ruptured the partnership between Paul and Barnabas (15:36-41).

Did the occurrence of sharp squabbles in the Antioch church demonstrate a lack of spirituality? Not necessarily. It probably demonstrated that here was a church—and leadership—willing to admit their differences and seek reconciliation rather than pretending these differences did not exist, and hoping they would fade away. The further a church advances, the greater the likelihood of disagreements and conflicts. Though the presence of problems may indicate carnality, at Antioch problems provided a path of progress against evil and error.

## Leader against Leader

This head-to-head encounter focused on two leading personalities in the New Testament. C. Peter Wagner calls the incident "one of the Scripture's best-known heavyweight fights." The title is deserved on two counts: not only are topflight "contenders" involved, but the "heaviness" of the issue concerns the heart of the Gospel.

• *Peter.* On one side we have Peter, generally recognized as number one among Jesus' twelve disciples, not without reason. He was named first on every list of the Twelve; he was their spokesman; he chaired the election of a successor to Judas; he was the fervent preacher on the Day of Pentecost; and he was the first to proclaim the Gospel to Gentiles in the house of Cornelius. Peter was involved in almost every significant action in the first twelve chapters of Acts except a few events involving Stephen and Philip.

• *Paul.* On the other side is the redoubtable Paul. As Peter fades from the pages of Acts, Paul enters as the dominant character. His journeys and journals comprise a major part of the New Testament. He wrote about half the New Testament books. In fact, outside the four Gospels, the first half of Acts, the Book of Revelation, and a few short letters, Paul's deeds and words make up the New Testament.

To debate who is the greater apostle might lead to the error of the Corinthian party spirit which stirs up believers in support of one human leader like fans cheering for a favorite quarterback.

Though we read much more about Paul than about Peter in the New Testament, we should not conclude that Peter's ministry diminishes after the First Church Council. From mid-Acts on, the Holy Spirit's purpose is to trace the outreach of the church across the Roman Empire through Paul and his helpers. Certainly Peter's place as foremost disciple during Jesus' earthly ministry, plus his forceful leadership during the early years of apostolic history, have established him near the pinnacle of biblical greatness. We must be careful not to overreact against certain church traditions which unscripturally elevate him to primacy.

We do not learn of Paul's rebuke of Peter in the historical record of Acts, but from Paul's report in his letter to the Galatians. He states, "But when Cephas (Peter) came to Antioch, I opposed him to his face, because he stood condemned" (Gal. 2:11, NASB). The reason Paul included this incident was that false teachers were questioning his authority by asserting his inferiority to the other disciples who had been trained by Jesus.

So Paul defends his special apostleship in the first two chapters of Galatians by three declarations.

First, Paul did not get his message from the other apostles, but by direct revelation from Jesus Christ (1:11-24).

Second, when Paul did consult with the "pillars" of the church at Jerusalem, including Apostles Peter and John many years after his dramatic conversion, Paul's beliefs were promptly acknowledged as the true Gospel (2:1-10).

Third—and this is the item under discussion in this chapter—when the Apostle Peter compromised the purity of the Gospel by his conduct, Paul rebuked him openly. This action placed Paul not only on an equality with Peter and the apostles but momentarily on a superior level. A rebuke to Peter by Paul or by anyone destroys any doctrine of Peter's infallibility or supremacy. Incidentally, here is the only post-Pentecost instance of an apostle rebuking an apostle.

## Reason for the Rebuke

At Antioch, Peter had been eating with Gentile believers and disregarding Jewish dietary laws. His conduct make it plain that Gentiles need not observe the Jewish traditions in order to be accepted by God. But when Jewish believers arrived from Jerusalem, Peter trimmed his sails. He avoided eating with the Gentiles in deference to the tradition-bound Jewish Christians. His old impulsive, vacillating streak, so frequently seen in the Gospels, surfaced again. In behaving so, he acted hypocritically. His actions spoke louder than words. He was saying by his practice what the Judaizers taught by precept: the Jewish food laws should be observed by "good Christians." How hard it is to change! Old habits cling tightly, even to apostles. Despite a special vision which prepared Peter to witness to the Gentile family of Cornelius—"God hath showed me that I should not call any man common or unclean" (Acts 10:28)—he yielded to human prejudice rather than God's direction. Paul quickly saw the inconsistency.

As usual, the leader's action carried others with it, even Barnabas who had been the encourager of the Gentile believers at Antioch from the beginning. The implications were staggering. Not only was a stigma of ceremonial uncleanness cast over Gentile Christians, but observers might conclude that obedience to the laws of Moses was indispensable for acceptance by God. Peter's action was an unintentional denial of the Gospel of grace. This fissure in basic doctrine could not be bridged by silence in hope of maintaining a spurious unity.

Scholars disagree as to whether this event took place before

41

or after the Jerusalem Council. But it seems likely to have occurred previously. Otherwise, Paul, in rebuking Peter, would have certainly referred to the council's verdict which as a written decree had been sent to all the churches of Antioch and vicinity (15:23). Peter's equivocating seems almost impossible after the council at which he firmly upheld salvation for Gentiles apart from what he called a "yoke" of the law upon the necks of the disciples (15:7-11).

## The Content of the Rebuke

Paul issued a strong rebuke, charging Peter with glaring inconsistency. Said Paul, "I withstood him to the face." Paul dug in with determined pugnacity. This is the same verb used by James when he tells us to resist the devil (James 4:7). And Paul flatly called Peter guilty, saying that "he was to be blamed" (Gal. 2:11).

Where the rebuke ends in Galatians 2 is difficult to determine, but Paul's commentary (2:14-18) gives the nature and explanation of the reproof. A reconstruction of the points shows the serious implications of Peter's action. Paul was saying, in effect, "Peter, you are returning to the Law, an intolerable burden which can never justify anyone."

Veteran Bible teacher Ralph L. Keiper paraphrases these verses graphically: "Peter, I smell ham on your breath. You forgot your Certs. There was a time when you wouldn't eat ham as part of your hope of salvation. Then after you trusted Christ, it didn't matter if you ate ham. But now when the no-ham eaters have come from Jerusalem you have gone back to your kosher ways. But the smell of ham still lingers on your breath. You are most inconsistent. You are compelling Gentile believers to observe Jewish law which can never justify anyone."

In essence, says Paul in Galatians 2:19-20, "By returning to the Law, you undercut strength for godly living. The Law gives no power to overcome sin. But by identifying with Christ, a person enters upon a new life. 'I am crucified with Christ . . . but Christ lives in me.' To return to the Law is to forsake the source of power—the indwelling Christ."

The final clause of the rebuke (or its commentary) makes a drastic claim. It charges Peter with making the death of Christ superfluous (2:21). If righteousness—the way to heaven and favorable standing with God—comes by keeping the Law, why did Christ come to earth to die? "Peter, you are going back to a system that rules out the cross of Christ; we could charge God with utmost cruelty in sending His Son to die if His death were unnecessary."

## Manner of the Rebuke

In this same Galatian letter Paul wrote, "Brethren, if a man be overtaken in a fault, ye which are spiritual, restore such an one in the spirit of meekness; considering thyself, lest thou also be tempted" (6:1). Paul did not hesitate to reprove his brother for a grievous fault, but he likely followed his own injunction and rebuked in a loving, caring manner.

Believers are commanded to admonish, exhort, reprimand, and correct one another—or figuratively, to wash one another's feet. Washing the saints' feet in a spiritual sense has come to mean helping our fellow Christians get rid of moral defilement accumulated in daily walk, as well as the more obvious lesson of lowly service to others.

As Paul "washed Peter's feet" in this particular circumstance, he followed procedures that are important for us in the same kind of service.

● *Make sure your brother's feet are actually dirty.* A young businesswoman arrived half an hour late to speak to a Bible study group. Immediately the friend who invited her took her aside and admonished her for keeping these first-time-attending, non-Christian neighbors waiting so long. Then the businesswoman explained, "My car was hit by a drunken driver. I could not leave till the police came; also I had to wait for a wrecker for my badly damaged car. I should have gone to the hospital, for I ache all over, but I refused the ambulance driver and got a taxi here."

We should never get the washbasin ready until we have the

facts straight. We should make sure our brother has definitely committed a trespass before attempting to correct him. Paul had full information on Peter's withdrawal from Gentile fellowship; he knew Peter's feet needed washing.

● *See that your own hands are clean.* In some sections of Scotland, bachelor friends of the bridegroom grab him the night before the wedding and carry him to a convenient spot where they remove his shoes and socks and pretend to wash his feet. But everyone has first blackened his hand with soot. Result—the groom's feet become dirtier than ever.

Whatever the significance of that custom, the person who tries to wash a fellow believer's feet with stains on his own hands will botch the job. Paraphrasing some advice of Jesus, "First wash your own hands, then you shall see clearly to wash your brother's feet."

In a Connecticut city fifty-three residents of a certain area signed a petition to stop reckless driving on their streets. The police set a watch. A few nights later five violators were caught. All five had signed the petition.

Paul's hands were clean in the matter of justification through faith apart from obedience to the works of the Law. He demonstrated his correctness of doctrine in the case of Titus. When pressure was exerted on Paul to circumcise Titus to make him acceptable as a convert to the Christian Hebrew church, Paul resisted in order to uphold the essential truth of the Gospel (Gal. 2:3-5). It is those "which are spiritual" who are to restore brethren that stumble.

● *Do foot washing in the proper place.* On some occasions foot-washing should be public. Private wrongs require private righting, whereas public wrongs demand public correction. For those who sin openly, the command is, "Rebuke before all" (1 Tim. 5:20). Since Peter's duplicity was public and widely influential, Paul's correction had to be "before them all" (Gal. 2:14).

The foot washer should never sound a trumpet before announcing, "I'm about to set Brother X straight." Foot washing is not an exhibition of dirt or failure. When renewal meetings at a Christian college led to open confession of sins that seemed to wallow in shame, the president wisely closed the service. We are to wash feet, not splatter mud around, thereby smearing reputations.

● *Have the water at proper temperature.* The water should be neither too hot nor too cold. Telling someone his faults with malice or glee makes the water boiling or freezing. A scolding becomes a scalding, or an icing. Though Paul, with his strong personality, had to guard against being overly harsh, here his rebuke seems to approximate the right temperature.

● *Stoop low.* To wash feet, you have to kneel as Jesus did to wash the disciples' feet. You cannot strut like a drill officer nor parade like a peacock when you're washing feet. Restoration should be done "considering thyself, lest thou also be tempted." We may assume that Paul's reproof was without a superior attitude, but with genuine humility before the Lord.

● *Handle gently.* When a person bares his soles, he is exposing a sensitive, tender, and ticklish part of his anatomy. That's why Paul said to restore in a spirit of gentleness.

John Wesley and a preacher-friend of plain habits were once invited to dinner where the host's daughter, noted for her beauty, had been profoundly impressed by Wesley's preaching. During a pause in the meal, Wesley's friend took the young woman's hand and called attention to the sparkling rings she wore. "What do you think of this, sir, for a Methodist hand?" The girl turned crimson. Wesley likewise was embarrassed, for his aversion to jewelry was only too well known. But with a benevolent smile, he simply said, "The hand is very beautiful." Wesley's remark both cooled the too-hot water poured by his friend, and made the foot-washing gentle. The young woman appeared at the evening service without her jewels, and became a strong Christian.

Someone said, "When you start heaving rocks of truth at people, be sure to wrap them in packages of love." Paul must have spoken the truth to Peter in love, though vigorously.

● *Dry them.* After the Lord washed the disciples' feet, He wiped them. An inadequate job of drying feet can cause the feet to become dirtier than before the washing when they contact dust. Restoring an erring brother involves drying his feet so he may again walk the paths of righteousness—we must forgive and forget.

In a Canadian church, an elder resigned from the board because of a brief lapse to his preconversion alcoholism. After years of sobriety, he had been seen intoxicated on a public vehicle. His resignation was noted in the official minutes of the elder board. Some months later at a midweek meeting, he confessed his failure and asked forgiveness of the church. He was soon voted back to the elder board. Not long after, the elders voted to expunge from their record every mention of the incident, so that today not a word of his indiscretion appears in the official minutes. That body of believers thoroughly dried the offender's feet.

F.B. Meyer, who suggested some of the above analogies in his book *Love to the Uttermost,* says: "We do not often enough wash one another's feet. We are conscious of the imperfections of those around us; we are content to note and criticize them. We dare not attempt to remove them, partly because we do not love with a love like Christ's, and partly because we are not willing to stoop low enough. None is able to restore those that are overtaken in a fault who does not count himself the chief of sinners and the least of saints. We need more of this lowly, loving spirit."

## The Outcome

How would Peter react to Paul's rebuke? It was a moment of major import. An ordinary leader could easily have reacted vehemently against Paul's criticism. Protecting his reputation could have triggered an angry defense despite the merits of the issue. And the church could have been split into two factions by a fierce collision of these two "heavyweight" leaders.

But Peter reacted, it seems, much the same way he had responded to previous reproofs. Peter characteristically acknowledged his error immediately and without reservation. The night before when he denied the Lord three times, the gaze of Jesus' eyes had been more than Peter could bear. He went out into the night, weeping in bitter remorse. Impetuous in his words and ways, he was just as hasty to mend his wrongs. Not a word indicates that he acted otherwise.

Peter's acceptance of Paul's rebuke is an example of how to receive a reprimand with Christian grace. In his heart Peter knew his action had been wrong and capable of doing great damage. It's likely he swallowed his pride and rejoined Gentile believers at mealtime that very day. Later, at the Jerusalem Council, Peter strongly supported Paul's position on salvation apart from keeping Moses' Law. Years later he wrote a letter in which he referred to "our beloved brother Paul" (2 Peter 3:15).

After the long, one-day, six-hour questioning of Tony Campolo when four panel members called on him to explain statements in one of his books, Campolo issued a statement that reflected a humble attitude. He wrote: "These brothers exercised 'tough love' and used our time together to build me up in Christ, correct me, and show me how to be more faithful to the Word of God. . . . This is good news for all of us who want to get on with the business of declaring the Good News."

Campolo's reaction is all the more remarkable since the panel failed to address the issue of whether or not he had been treated fairly. Campolo's associates felt they had an agreement that this question would be discussed: "Was the cancellation of Tony Campolo from Youth Congress '85 on theological grounds justified?" Whatever, Campolo emerged from the fracas to continue his dynamic ministry.

Who was the winner of the Paul-Peter heavyweight bout? There was no contest. Because Peter put up no fight, Paul carried the day. The contest that was avoided permitted the ongoing flow of the pure Gospel. The decision—both Peter and Paul were winners. And the entire church won as well.

# 4.

# The First Church Council

In 1985 popular literature professor Thomas Howard made public his conversion to Roman Catholicism and resigned from the faculty of Gordon College, Wenham, Massachusetts. It was no surprise to the college, for Howard had several months prior informed school officials of his intention to become a Catholic, and the college faculty senate had begun an examination of Catholic doctrine and had met with Howard on two occasions. In time, the senate had issued a 15-page report which concluded that Roman Catholic doctrine is incompatible with Gordon College's doctrinal statement, which is unmistakably Protestant and Reformed in character, and which Gordon College professors must sign. The report noted that, though Catholics and Protestants hold much in common within the historic Christian tradition, serious doctrinal differences do remain between the two confessing communities.

Gordon College's faculty senate is just one of hundreds of boards, assemblies, associations, alliances, federations, fellowships, consultations, leagues, conferences, conventions, convocations, vestries, presbyteries, committees, cabinets, congresses, and councils through the centuries that have met to determine doctrinal, liturgical, and constitutional correctness. At first, in the early centuries synods met locally, then developed into diocesan, then metropolitan, then patriachal, then finally into large ecumenical councils, authoritative to the whole church. Church historians list eight ecumenical councils from A.D. 325–869, convened by emperors to handle doctrinal interests.

But the granddaddy of all such gatherings, though limited territorially, was an assembly convened in Jerusalem between Paul's first and second missionary journeys, commonly known as the First Church Council, mentioned previously. Its story is told in Acts 15.

## A Chronic Contention

Today most churches are composed exclusively of Gentile believers. In fact, many church members have never met a Jewish Christian. But in the early church the situation was the reverse, for in the first two decades of Christianity practically all believers were Jewish. From the beginning Jewish believers found it difficult to accept Gentile converts, even though the Great Commission, repeatedly given the apostles during the ten-day post-Resurrection period, specified carrying the Gospel to all nations (Matt. 28:19; Mark 16:15; Luke 24:47; Acts 1:8). Though among the disciples who heard this universal command, Peter had to be prepared by a heaven-sent vision to accept an invitation to preach to non-Jews at Caesarea (Acts 10:9-29). When he returned from his mission to the household of the Roman soldier Cornelius, the church leaders at Jerusalem called him on the carpet. At first sharply critical, they finally accepted his explanation and praised God that salvation had been granted to the Gentiles (11:18).

When Gentiles at Antioch in Syria began to join the new Hebrew-Christian church there, the surprised Jerusalem church sent Barnabas to investigate. So many more Gentiles believed on Christ that Barnabas sought Paul's help to instruct them. Later, sent out by this largely Gentile church to evangelize Asia Minor, Barnabas and Paul won hundreds of Gentiles to Christ. When reports of the influx reached the Jerusalem church, some Jews found it difficult to accept Gentiles as spiritual equals. They revered Moses' laws and expected Christianity to retain its Old Testament heritage.

Up at Antioch no disharmony existed till Judaizing teachers from Jerusalem arrived. This party of Christians, who had previously belonged to a sect of the Pharisees, could not reconcile themselves to the admission of the Gentiles unless the Gentiles were first circumcised (15:1).

The issue was indeed critical. Either a person was saved by faith alone, or by faith plus the meritorious ceremony of circumcision. If the latter, the Gospel of grace was virtually revoked. Paul and Barnabas recognized this as a battle for Christian liberty, the very crux of the Reformation struggle to be fought fifteen centuries later. There Luther's text from Romans, "The just shall live by faith" (1:17), ruled out the addition of penance, indulgences, priestly intercession, human deeds, or rites of any kind as a basis of acceptance by God.

Paul and Barnabas had seen a host of Gentiles won to Christ apart from keeping Mosaic Law. With the missionary movement expected to penetrate farther into Gentile territory, this heresy would have to be handled before any more evangelistic tours could be started. No doctrinal controversy could be more serious.

## Referral to a Sister Fellowship
Though most churches handle their own affairs, seeking advice from the larger fellowship on an overwhelming problem is a sign of strength, not weakness. Churches of like precious faith associate today for purposes of fellowship, appointment of and report on missionaries, advice on ordination of pastors, building or approval of schools, the passing of resolutions on current affairs, and sometimes consultation on grave and difficult situations.

In the summer of 1975 a group of Christian leaders met in a Minneapolis hotel to consider what the *New York Times* called the first major controversy to strike the charismatic movement. The center of contention was an alleged network of disciples linked by doctrine and loyalty in hierarchical fashion to a Florida-based organization. Leaders of the organization stressed the need to disciple converts to maturity, but opponents claimed the methods promoted doctrinal and financial control by the leadership over their followers. It is commendable, as in the Antiochan-Jerusalem conference, that consultation proceeded with sincere concern and wholesome atmosphere.

More recently, when the PTL organization desperately stood in need of help, they sought the counsel of a total outsider in the person of Jerry Falwell, who formed a new board to try to steer it through difficult days.

So, the church at Antioch, vexed by the insistence on circumcision by the Jerusalem teachers, "determined that Paul and Barnabas, and certain other of them, should go up to Jerusalem unto the apostles and elders about this question (Acts 15:2).

Though often referred to as the First Church Council, theologian Frederic Farrar rejected that title. Bible teacher G. Campbell Morgan commented: "He showed that the council at Jerusalem was not a convention of delegates, but a meeting of the church at Jerusalem to receive a deputation from the church at Antioch, and to consider a subject of grave importance in the matter of missionary enterprise. He pointed out, moreover, that this gathering in Jerusalem was for purposes of consultation, and not for final and dogmatic decision. Almost all councils subsequent to the first have attempted to fix some habit of ritual, or to give final form to the expression of some great truth. Neither of these things was attempted in the gathering in Jerusalem" (*The Acts of the Apostles*, Fleming H. Revell, 1924, p. 355).

In rebuttal, many would point out that the deputation sent from Antioch did seem to have the status of delegates, also that a decision was rendered on a great truth and expressed in written form. In the minds of many the event deserves the title of council. Perhaps that's why so many commentators refer to it as such.

## Why Go to Jerusalem?

Wasn't Antioch a close second to the mother church both in numbers and influence? Might not this conference degenerate into a battle between a Gentile church and a Jewish church? Paul and Barnabas were sent because what was desired was not an Antioch-versus-Jerusalem contest, but an Antiochan-Jerusalem consensus on this crucial issue.

Since Jerusalem had the Gospel first, its real genius should be understood by Christians there. Also, since the apostles there could speak most authoritatively about the true Gospel, no higher court could be appealed to. And as Jerusalem was both the source and the stronghold of the error, vindication there of Paul's teaching would purify the stream of Christian proclamation.

Arriving at Jerusalem, the delegation from Antioch was welcomed by the church, the apostles and the elders. Barnabas and Paul reported God's marvelous deeds through their ministry, doubtless highlighting the conversion of Gentiles. But some believing Pharisees objected and said in effect, "Go back and tell those Gentiles that if they want full admission into the church they must submit to the Law of Moses and the covenant of circumcision" (vv. 4-5).

Sensing the importance of the dispute, the apostles and elders called a special meeting of the church.

## A Solemn Conclave

Whatever preliminary or private sessions may have been held, the whole membership ("all the multitude") was present for the major discussion (v. 12). Luke gives a summary of what happened.

 • *Lesser leaders.* Apparently unnamed leaders spoke first, some on each side of the question, with "much disputing" (v. 7).

 • *Peter.* More mature and rocklike than in his younger days, Peter kept silent as the debate went back and forth. Then he rose and said that God had decided the question some time back when the Gentile family of Cornelius had been saved by faith and given the Holy Spirit just as had happened to the believing Jews. Why tempt God, asked Peter, by adding to Gentile shoulders a yoke even Jewish forefathers found an impossible burden? There is but one way—"through grace"— for both Jew and Gentile (vv. 7-11).

So strong was the impact of Peter's words that silence reigned.

● *Barnabas and Paul.* Barnabas spoke next, before Paul, because Barnabas had been well-known in Jerusalem long before Paul's conversion. They added their testimony to Peter's about God's redeeming workings among the Gentiles (v. 12).

Again there was quiet, so convincing was the combined witness of Peter, Barnabas and Paul. Then came time for the chairman, James, to speak. Apparently the leader of the church, James supported Peter's testimony, then pointed out that Gentile response to the Gospel fulfilled Old Testament prophecy, and had been God's plan from ages past (vv. 13-18).

## The Verdict

James summed up all the debate, reports, and discussion, then gave his judgment: "We should not make it difficult for the Gentiles who are turning to God" (v. 19, NIV). In essence, "Don't ask Gentiles to keep the Law or be circumcised in order to be saved!" This judicious verdict upheld the unadulterated Gospel; namely, that a person is saved by faith in Christ apart from the works or the rites of the Law.

James is sometimes accused of contradicting Paul because of his emphasis on works in his epistle (James 2:17, 20, 24, 26). But at the Jerusalem conference, James and Paul agree 100 percent that works are not necessary for salvation.

Instructively, the verdict of the council was not decided by a vote of the participants. Facts are facts regardless of people's opinions, and the apostles knew the facts. Some children watching a calf frisking around a field argued whether it was a "boy or a girl calf." Finally one child piped up, "I know how we can tell; let's vote on it." But the truth of animal gender or doctrinal reality is not decided by poll-taking. Paul would have rejected any decision at that conference that denied the Gospel of grace revealed to him by Christ, as he emphasized in the epistle to the Galatian church (Gal. 1:6-9). Paul's purpose for the consultation was to elicit from the Jerusalem leaders a reaffirmation of a truth already established but which was under attack by the Judaizers.

Similarly, if any church conclave today makes an official affirmation downgrading any major fundamental like the Virgin Birth of Christ, His deity, His substitutionary atonement, His bodily resurrection, His personal coming again, or the full inspiration of the Scriptures, that declaration must be immediately and thoroughly rejected by those who would remain loyal to revealed, historic Christianity. No church council can add to, subtract from, or change in any way divinely inscripturated biblical truth.

At a denominational convention in Ottawa, Canada, in October 1919, a pastor who introduced a resolution in defense of a certain biblical truth was told that the convention deplored controversy because the Christian church scored its victories only as controversy was avoided. To which the pastor replied, "Ever heard of Luther, Knox, or Calvin?"

## Conciliation

If the Judaizers had been counting on James with his strong Jewish background to render a verdict in favor of circumcision, they were sadly disillusioned. However, James added his recommendation for Gentile believers' conduct that urged compliance with the Old Testament moral law. Gentiles were to abstain from idolatry, from fornication, "from what is strangled," and "from blood." At first examination it seems that one of these prohibitions is ceremonial—"from what is strangled." However, many manuscripts omit "from what is strangled," which would then make all the prohibitions come from the moral law: idolatry, fornication, and bloodshed (murder). Thus while James was opposed to placing the yoke of Jewish ceremonialism on the necks of Gentile believers, he was not excusing them from obedience to the great moral commands.

On the other hand, if James' list of prohibitions did in fact include a ceremonial Law—namely, avoidance of things strangled—then Gentile abstention would enhance fellowship, ease suspicious fears of the Jewish community, and cement peace among the brethren. In later decades the ritualistic scruples would become less relevant.

James' compromise was paralleled later by Paul's principle of surrendering certain liberties that would mislead a weaker brother. Both were loving measures prescribed for the good of the whole church.

A devout German couple who had imbibed beer and wine socially with their Christian friends in the old country discovered after moving to the eastern U.S. that their new Christian friends frowned on alcohol as a beverage. The couple graciously surrendered their old practice. Their discarded habit had broken no law, but did wound Christian love.

## Delivery of the Verdict

The "whole church" shared in the ratification and sending of the verdict (Acts 15:22).

• *Sent representatives.* When the Antioch delegation returned to their home church, the Jerusalem church graciously sent along with them two of their own "chief men," Judas Barnabas and Silas, both prophets, as their representatives (vv. 22-23). The caliber of these messengers would reinforce the authenticity of the verdict they carried.

• *Wrote a letter.* The verdict was put in writing. Here is a letter not listed in the index of New Testament epistles. It could be titled *To the Gentiles in Antioch, Syria, and Cilicia* (v. 23). Authors were the apostles, elders, and the entire church at Jerusalem. The salutation is found only in one other New Testament epistle, that of James, which hints at his involvement in its composition.

The letter, which summarized the council, contained these salient points:

— disavowal of any backing for the Judaizing teachers
— unity of the Jerusalem church on the verdict

— recognition of Barnabas and Paul as beloved brothers
— contents to be confirmed personally by messengers
— law-keeping not necessary for salvation
— list of concessions the Gentiles should make

● *Brought joy.* When the letter was read at Antioch, the congregation "rejoiced" (v. 31). What a relief to have so vital a matter decided in keeping with the simplicity of the Gospel.

## The Outcome

● *Antioch church strengthened.* The two prophets stayed a while to encourage the brethren. Had there been no conflict, the church at Antioch would have missed the ministry of these Jerusalem leaders.

● *Harmony deepened.* After completing their mission, the two delegates returned to Jerusalem with the blessing of the Antioch church, which dismissed them "in peace" (v. 33). The relationship between the two churches had never been better.

● *Work advanced.* Doubtless Paul would have preferred engaging in church planting than in disputing with fellow Christians during those days. But the desirable had to be sacrificed to the unpleasant in order to maintain the truth of the Gospel. With the official backing of the Jerusalem church, Paul could proceed full steam ahead, proclaiming to the ends of the Empire the liberating news, "A man is justified by faith without the deeds of the law" (Rom. 3:28).

● *United front.* After the partnership of Paul and Barnabas severed, Paul chose Silas as his co-worker. A more propitious choice could not have been made. Wherever they went, Paul's message of forgiveness through faith was seconded by Silas, a leader from the Jewish-oriented Jerusalem church, and one of the two representatives of the council to carry the verdict. Together Paul and Silas delivered that decision to churches along the way (Acts 16:4-5). All the apostles and their associates would preach the one and only Gospel.

## Church Councils

The early church fleshed out its doctrines at large councils from the third on through the sixth century. The first of these, called the Council of Nicea (A.D. 325), settled the dispute over the full deity of Christ. Arius, a pastor in Alexandria, taught that Jesus Christ was not the true God, and was neither eternal nor omnipotent. He was a created being and a half-God. Bishop Alexander would have none of it and called a synod at Alexandria which excommunicated Arius and condemned his teaching. When Arius won some friends among church leaders for his views, Emperor Constantine knew the matter had to be defused, so he called for a council to meet at Nicea.

Bruce L. Shelley in *Church History in Plain Language* (Word, 1982, p. 115) comments, "What a vivid picture that first imperial synod made! Most of the 300 or so bishops had fresh memories of the days of persecution. Many could show the scars of suffering and prison. One had lost an eye during the persecution. Another had lost the use of his hands under torture. But the days of suffering seemed over now. The bishops did not set out for Nicea secretly, as they used to do, fearing arrest. They did not painfully walk the long miles as once they did. They rode in comfort to the council, all their expenses paid, the guests of the emperor."

Sitting in the center of the conference hall, Constantine presided over the early sessions, a glittering figure in his imperial, jewel-encrusted robes. When it came time for the doctrinal issue, he stepped aside, committing the resolution to the church leaders. In opposition to Arianism, which lost the struggle, there emerged the Nicean Creed, declaring the full deity of Jesus Christ, and to this day a standard of orthodoxy among Roman, Eastern, Anglican, and other churches.

The Council of Constantinople in A.D. 381 affirmed the full humanity of Jesus. The Council of Ephesus in A.D. 431 and the Council of Chalcedon in A.D. 451 asserted the two natures of Christ, one human and one divine, in a unified Person.

The canon, with the list of New Testament books as we have them today, was published in the Councils of North Africa at Hippo (A.D. 393) and at Carthage (A.D. 397). Says Shelley,

"They were only recognizing those writings that had made their authority felt in the churches. The shape of the New Testament shows that the early churches' primary aim was to submit fully to the teachings of the apostles. In that purpose they shaped the character of Christianity for all time. The faith remained catholic precisely because it was apostolic" (ibid., p. 83).

Basic doctrines, like the deity of Christ, justification by faith, and the authority of Scripture cannot be negotiated or compromised. However, the Jew-Gentile issue with some parallel to the First Church Council situation has surfaced in recent times. Many Jewish believers today want to retain enriching Jewish distinctives. The spreading Christian messianic movement in the U.S. is inclined toward calling meeting places synagogues and its ministers rabbis, conducting services Friday night, using Jewish terms like "Yeshua" instead of "Jesus," celebrating Jewish holidays, observing Bar Mitzvahs, and in some cases wanting to be known as the fourth branch of Judaism (with Orthodox, Conservative, and Reform). This emphasis on Jewishness caused the sixty-year-old Hebrew Christian Alliance of America to change its name to the Messianic Jewish Alliance. The purpose was to gain a wider hearing of the Gospel and its already-come Messiah.

Without question, no Jewish practice or rite should be added to faith as essential for salvation. On the other hand, wise concessions can be made for a more palatable and understandable witness to the Jewish community. If talented Jewish music or drama groups can capture the attention of their own people and help them appreciate their Jewishness and also teach Gentile congregations to sing Messiah's praise with Jewish rhythm, perhaps a new day for Jewish evangelism is around the corner.

## Leadership of the Holy Spirit and Prayer

The early chapters of Acts frequently report the believers in one accord in one place in prayer (1:14; 4:24). Prayer and unity seem to go together. United prayer can do much to stave off rifts and splits, and create a sense of oneness. A spirit of unity seemed to brood over that First Church Council. The official letter announcing the council's verdict stated, "It seemed good unto us, being assembled with one accord, to send chosen men unto you" (15:25). Then three verses later, the letter says this, "It seemed good to the Holy Spirit and to us" (v. 28, NIV). Unity in prayer brings the mind of the Spirit. When the Spirit's leadership is followed, calm supplants storm and blessing banishes battle.

Dr. G. Campbell Morgan commented, "We must freely admit we very seldom hear this language. We do read that a matter was carried by an overwhelming majority, but that is a very different thing. An overwhelming majority often leaves behind it a minority disaffected and dangerous. We shall come to unanimity when we are prepared to discuss freely [and] frankly our absolute differences, on the basis of a common desire to know the mind of the Lord. If we come . . . having made our minds up that so it must be, then we hinder the Holy Spirit, and make it impossible for Him to make known His mind and will. But if we come, perfectly sure in our minds, but wanting to know what the Lord's mind is, then ere the council ends, today as yesterday, the moment will come when we shall be able to say with a fine dignity and a splendid force, 'It seems good to the Holy Spirit and to us' " (*The Acts of the Apostles,* p. 365).

Before sending out their first missionaries, the church at Antioch had fasted and prayed. Later when the Judaizing error was detected, the church doubtless again went to prayer and fasting. They were concerned over the controversy and potential division. As a result, the council was held. Church doctrine was more clearly delineated. A damaging rift was averted. And the believers in all churches were drawn closer together.

# 5.

# Sharp Split
# between Leaders

Dr. Harold Ockenga and Dr. Carl McIntyre were close in their student days, both leaving Princeton Seminary because of its modernism, and both enrolling in the newly formed Westminster Seminary. In fact, each was a member of the other's wedding party. People who recall their early association often comment how sad that such good friends should have turned out to be so widely separated through most of their remaining years. Ockenga went on to sparkplug the formation of the National Association of Evangelicals, an organization which McIntyre repeatedly attacked through the years as a compromising organization because of its alleged weak position on so-called apostate denominations. As a protest to the NAE, McIntyre started the American Council of Churches, which demanded complete separation from all groups associated in any way with liberalism. Comrades in the Lord's work in the early years, Ockenga and McIntyre were sharply divided in their later ministries.

Back in the early 1900s when the tongues movement began to sweep across the U.S., many Christian and Missionary Alliance branches accepted Pentecostal teaching. But in April 1910, Dr. A.B. Simpson, founder of the C & MA and editor of its official publication, wrote an editorial opposing the teaching "that this special gift is for all or is the evidence of the Baptism of the Holy Ghost. Nor can we receive or use to edification in our work and assemblies those who press these extreme and unscriptural views."

His position cost the Alliance dearly. The recent book *All for Jesus*, a delightfully readable account of the 100 years of C&MA history, quotes Dr. William W. Menzies, an Assemblies of God historian: "Several great churches in the Alliance, and numerous outstanding ministers, reluctantly parted company with the parent body when the Pentecostal testimony was stifled by the Alliance leadership. Such 'come-outers' provided a substantial proportion of early Assemblies of God leadership" (Robert L. Niklaus, John S. Sawin, Samuel J. Stoesz, Christian Publications, 1986, p. 115). This parting of the way became inevitable and painful, especially for Dr. Simpson.

These episodes were not the first time Christian leaders have parted, for one reason or another, down through the centuries. Some 1900 years ago Paul and Barnabas split over the desertion of a young assistant, John Mark. Paul was inclined to be tough on the youthful defector, while Barnabas preferred the tender approach. The sharp contention caused an unresolved clash between these spiritual giants. This incident affords insights into understanding and solving conflicts between Christian brethren today.

## Godly Men May Have Opposing Views
Paul and Barnabas, two of the best-known New Testament leaders, both called apostles, and close co-workers in pastoral and missionary ministries, found themselves at odds over the best way to do the Lord's work. In fact, so firm were their differing convictions and so fierce their contention that they split into separate ways.

This painful separation shows the humanity of these apostles, as men of limited wisdom and imperfect character. Never should we set a human being on a pedestal, as an idol to usurp the place of Jesus, who alone is our unblemished example.

Early church leaders were not stained-glass characters, but flesh-and-blood mortals who had quarrels which could lead to hot temper and consequent coolness. Their short-lived altercation does not detract from our admiration of their overall ministry. God will reward them for their enduring devotion, which so overshadows their temporary dissension. Their failures remind us that God uses fallible people to do His sacred work. The Holy Spirit does not gild the lily.

Dr. G. Campbell Morgan expressed appreciation for this lack of whitewash: "I am greatly comforted whenever I read this. I am thankful for the revelation of the humanity of these men. If I had never read that Paul and Barnabas had a contention, I should have been afraid. These men were not angels, but they were men" (*Acts of the Apostles*, p. 369).

Through the centuries sincere Christian people have stood on opposite sides of many issues. What is vital in every disagreement is openness to God's leading and love for the disputant. Christians who disagree honestly and peaceably can still serve God honorably.

## Each Side May Have a Valid Point

After the Jerusalem Council, Paul suggested to Barnabas that they visit the churches they had established on their first missionary journey to see how the converts were doing. Barnabas agreed, adding that he wished to take Mark along. Mention of the name of Mark raised a red flag before Paul because on that first journey Mark had abandoned the team in Asia Minor (Acts 13:5, 13). The suitability or pseudoability of Mark for further ministry was the bone of contention.

Why did Mark defect? Did he return to Jerusalem because he was homesick, or had a girlfriend there? Or was his mother, likely a widow, somewhat dependent on him, even though well-to-do? Or did Mark resent Paul taking over the leadership from his cousin Barnabas? (Col. 4:10) (Interestingly, mention of Mark's defection is found in the sentence which gives the first indication of Paul's primacy on the team. Acts 13:13 speaks of "Paul and his company," omitting Barnabas' name entirely. Thereafter the order is more frequently "Paul and Barnabas.") Or, as they branched out to strong Gentile territory in Asia Minor, was Mark, close friend of apostle-to-the-Jews Peter, not yet sympathetic with Paul's readiness to preach the Gospel to the Gentiles? Or was Mark afraid of what was ahead—rugged, robber-infested country, unfriendly reception, even persecution? Had his youthfulness gotten the better of him, showing that he was just not yet ready for rigorous missionary activity, perhaps running ahead of God's will for his life?

Because of this defection, for whatever reason, Paul refused to take Mark on this next trip. But Barnabas insisted on Mark's coming. Who was right? Each had sound, strong reasoning for his position. As countless believers have done through the centuries in numerous committee, board, or business meetings in churches the world over, Paul and Barnabas discussed the matter. Let's imagine their possible dialogue.

PAUL:    Mark? We can't take him. He failed us last time.

BARNABAS:    But that was last time.

PAUL:    He's likely to fail us again. He's a deserter.

BARNABAS:    He's had time to think it over. We've got to give him another chance. He's got the makings of a great missionary.

PAUL:    Tell me, Barnabas, isn't it because he's your cousin that you want to take him again?

BARNABAS:    That's not fair. You know I've tried to help many people who aren't related to me. I'm convinced this lad needs understanding and encouragement. He could be a great evangelist some day.

PAUL: We need someone who can stand up to persecution, an angry mob, beatings, perhaps jail. Our team has to be close-knit, thoroughly reliable. How can we trust a lad who failed like Mark? No, Barnabas. Recall the word of the Master, "No man who puts his hand to the plow and looks back is fit for the kingdom of God."

BARNABAS: I've talked to him about his failure. I'm sure he won't defect again. To refuse him might do spiritual damage at the moment of his repentance. It'd be like breaking a bruised reed, like quenching smoking flax.

PAUL: It's too soon to trust him.

BARNABAS: Paul, remember how soon after your conversion I took a chance on you. The apostles were afraid of you, thinking you were faking your conversion in order to infiltrate the church at Jerusalem. I didn't make you prove yourself first. I'd rather not keep Mark waiting. I vouch for him now.

Each had a strong argument. Paul thought the *ministry* to eternal souls would be jeopardized by softness to Mark. Barnabas deemed that the *man*, a potential disciple, would be endangered by severity.

How often the same type of conflict surfaces in church life: the *ministry* versus the *man*, the *work* versus the *worker*, the *principle* versus the *person*. A Sunday School teacher is needed for a high-school class. When a name is suggested, some object because he is too new a Christian and could harm the students' development. But others point out he has matured much since his conversion and would grow considerably through this assignment. Partisans take sides, sometimes with ill feelings, one group thinking of the caliber of *performance*, the other of the spiritual growth of the *person*.

Some think Barnabas may have been guilty of nepotism, a practice defined by the dictionary as favoritism shown a relative, such as giving an appointive job on the basis of relationship. Interestingly, nepotism comes from the word "nephew."

Whether or not Barnabas was influenced, either consciously or unconsciously, by his family connection to Mark, there's no way of knowing. But denominational leaders often caution churches against putting relatives of church members on the payroll, especially on the pastoral staff; and they believe it is definitely unwise for a relative of the pastoral staff to serve on the church board. Dr. Russell A. Shive, for many years general director of the Conservative Baptist Association of America, gives the following reasons for not putting church members' relatives on the staff:

Family ties are usually stronger than objective analysis, so when a staff member's relative is censured or disciplined by a church, the pastor, despite how he stands on the matter, may end up in a cool relationship with the staff person.

If a staff person is dismissed because of inefficiency, embarrassed and angry relatives may cause members to take sides over the issue, or even leave the church themselves.

Tension is heightened if people think a staff member is getting special treatment in the area of salary, vacation, or amount of responsibility, because of family ties.

Shive thinks that when a close relative of the pastor comes on the staff, such as his son as assistant, problems are not as quick to arise because people regard the son as an extension of his father. However, building a family dynasty has its dangers. Also, when a single person from the outside joins the staff and marries into a church family, objectivity suffers somewhat.

## Seeking Wise Compromise

Members of one growing church confessed: "Sure, we've had disagreements about the size of the pulpit, the order of service, choice of staff members, and some very serious matters, but still we don't lose control and disrupt the Lord's work. Always some folks concede a little to help reach a satis-factory decision."

Could Paul or Barnabas, or both, have developed a reason-able compromise? Giving in would not have meant heresy, for no doctrine was involved. Could Paul have said, "We'll tell him he's on probation. If he doesn't work out the first month, we'll ship him home again." After all, Paul would later write about love that suffers long.

Or perhaps Barnabas could have conceded, "We do need dedicated workers on our team. Let's give Mark a minor as-signment to see how he does. Meanwhile we'll start on our journey and, if we hear he's measuring up, we'll send for him to join us along the way." A player usually proves himself in the minors before he's called up to the majors.

Or could they have agreed on a contingent plan? "Let's take Mark, but others also. If Mark deserts us again, we'll have others to fall back on." Either the inventiveness of love should have discovered some middle ground, or the submis-sion of love should have yielded the point entirely. Both surely subscribed to the truth of "submitting yourselves one to another in the fear of God" (Eph. 5:21). Why didn't they prac-tice it?

Let's return to the new Christian suggested as teacher for the high-school Sunday School class. Because some thought he was not spiritually mature enough, a compromise solution could let the candidate substitute-teach for a month or two, or be given some exposure in a helping role with that age group. Evaluation of his performance would give both sides a better basis for a decision.

A growing church which attracted a wide spectrum of be-lievers disagreed over the kind of worship for the Sunday morning service. Guitar music, folk tunes, and talk-back ser-mons were creeping into what had been a rather dignified affair. The old-timers wanted the formal service restored. Po-larization was developing. The two groups met to seek the Spirit's wisdom and happily accepted a proposal to devote the evening service to contemporary worship forms, returning the morning hour to the traditional style. Someone commented facetiously, "In the morning, it's Bach; in the evening, it's rock." A prayerful and submissive spirit helped bring a satisfying solution for both parties.

Paul was endorsed by the church at Antioch as he left with his new partner, Silas, but such endorsement for Barnabas is not mentioned (Acts 15:40). Some conclude that the church took Paul's side, but the omission may only indicate that the record from here on focuses on Paul. The argument from silence is not conclusive in this case.

## Keeping Their Cool in the Heat

Neither Paul nor Barnabas would submit to the other. Both were obstinate. Paul remained adamant in his principle that one who had so failed should not be trusted so soon again. His position hardened into stern intolerance of the weakness of this youth.

On the other hand, Barnabas, who every time he appears in the Holy Writ is helping someone, wanted to help a defector back into the swing of service. He was determined to give Mark another chance.

Could not Paul have tempered his severity, and Barnabas his softness? But these men remained firm, clashing head-on.

The main part of the Greek word used to describe the apostles' contention means "sharp." In its compound form it gives us our English "paroxysm." The Septuagint (Greek translation of the Old Testament) used this word to describe the great indignation which led God to root Israel out of its land (Deut. 29:28). Doctor Luke, the author of this incident in Acts, well knew that this medical word was used of a sudden seizure, spasm, or the point at which a disease took a turn for the worse, breaking forth in its severest form. The altercation between Paul and Barnabas broke into acute, fierce form. Personal feelings ran high. Even big-hearted, lovable Barnabas used loud words.

Discussion and disagreement are inevitable, but losing one's "cool" is wrong. In beginning to raise one's voice, one should be careful that he's making a point of argument, not manifesting anger or contempt. A sign of spiritual as well as emotional maturity is the ability to argue without losing self-control. God's cause is never prospered by temper tantrums. "The wrath of man worketh not the righteousness of God" (James 1:20). The Lord may have permitted their splitting, but He was not pleased with their spatting. Could they not have disagreed calmly instead of with cutting contention?

A man involved in a dispute which led to a break with another officer in a missionary organization later admitted long-lasting regret at inaccurate accusations he made in the heat of temper.

## God Can Bless Division

With each insisting on his own way, Paul and Barnabas parted company, sadly ending their close partnership of around ten years. Barnabas went first, sailing with Mark to Cyprus, familiar territory to Mark, which made it easier for him to take up the reins of dedication. Paul headed into Asia Minor with Silas, leader from the Jerusalem church, to strengthen the churches established on Paul's first journey (Acts 15:22, 39-41).

When two strong persons or factions find themselves diametrically and unalterably opposed, the best solution may be separation so each can wholeheartedly pursue his own objective. An unresolvable difference is often best served by amicable, sensitive sundering.

Peter Wagner, in his book *Leading Your Church to Growth*, points out that Paul's missionary band was quite different from New Testament churches: "He maintained high requirements for joining and monitored the work of the members. He could and did fire those who were incompetent, with John Mark being the most obvious case. Because it was a task-oriented structure and Mark was not contributing well to the task, out he went. The task was more important than the person. Barnabas soon went too, after it was obvious that he and Paul weren't seeing the issues eye to eye. Disharmony among top leadership is not tolerated in the sodality (missionary-oriented

69

structure). Why? It stands in the way of goal accomplishment. Notice that Mark was not excommunicated from the congregational structure because it is people-oriented and not task-oriented" (Regal, 1984, p. 149).

Though the friction between Paul and Barnabas was unpleasant and regrettable, their break-up proved productive, bringing blessing in disguise. Because God can make angry men praise Him, divine providence can override a division so as to yield compensating dividends. Contrary to the ecumenical desire for church union, a division of forces may further the Lord's work.

● *Two teams.* With two Gospel teams, Barnabas-Mark and Paul-Silas, the work was extended so that more churches were founded and more souls won. Church-growth leader C. Peter Wagner points out that clashes between dynamic new leaders and settled old pastors in Latin American churches have resulted in what has been termed "growth by splitting." Says Wagner: "No one will say that church splits are intrinsically good. They frequently involve nasty quarrels and legal hassles. Often they leave broken hearts and permanent enemies behind. Nevertheless, God promises that all things work together for good to them that love Him (Rom. 8:28). Strangely enough, church splits among Pentecostals have frequently resulted in accelerated growth for both sides of the split" (*Look Out, the Pentecostals Are Coming,* Creation House, p. 62).

Church history records numerous divisions between leaders, churches, and organizations, some rancid and jarring, others sweet and gentle. Sadly, some developed because of fractious personalities; others were spurred by important principles. Also, innumerable Christians have severed associations on good terms in order to take up different kinds of ministry incompatible with their former patterns and partners, but conformed to what they believe is God's plan. Countless churches and dozens of denominations have been born through irreconcilable contention.

In 1860 the bearded Jonathan Blanchard, first president of

Wheaton College, west of Chicago, organized a campus church independent of the college, known as the College Church of Christ, and affiliated with the Congregational denomination. Sixty-nine years later, Dr. J. Oliver Buswell, then president of Wheaton College, took action to disassociate the church from the denomination, which he labeled as liberal. Not everyone saw eye to eye with him. So after prayer and discussion, Dr. Buswell led a group of College Church members to start a new church, known today as the Wheaton Bible Church. The fiftieth anniversary booklet of the Wheaton Bible Church commented, "As history has borne out, the 1929 separation was another Paul and Barnabas case, which, despite intense feelings on both sides, God used to His glory, abundantly blessing both congregations down through the years." Today both churches thrive with large congregations and evident divine blessing. The College Church of Christ, however, is like the Wheaton Bible Church, now independent, having years ago broken its denominational ties.

Does all this endorse ecclesiastical altercations in order to multiply churches, missionary societies, and Christian organizations? A thousand times—no! The peace of a church and of a Christian organization is very important. Church or Christian organization clashes all too often bring disrepute to Christ's cause and sometimes disaster to the participants. A small Christian day school in an eastern state, through conflict, separated into two smaller Christian day schools, neither of which was able to survive. Only God's grace, in union or division, produces progress.

● *Two areas.* The two teams headed for different localities, perhaps as a conciliatory move or a first-century harmonious comity arrangement. With Barnabas and Mark in Cyprus, and Paul and Silas in Asia Minor, at least they didn't start churches in each other's backyard as some splitting congregations have been known to do in our day. An executive who broke with a mission whose headquarters were on the East coast wisely established his new office in Texas.

● *Rift healed.* At first, both likely suffered embarrassing

71

moments when old friends on Cyprus asked Barnabas,
"Where's Paul?" and in Asia Minor asked Paul, "How come
Barnabas isn't with you?" These two wonderful men could not
remain at odds. Barnabas, so warm toward people, and Paul
who wrote "the greatest of these is love" would reach out
toward each other. A few years later Paul referred kindly to
Barnabas in one of his letters (1 Cor. 9:6). Though they did
not resume their partnership, the sharp contention did yield to
the gentle persuasion of love as they kept up on each other's
ministry, their paths doubtless crossing on occasion.

• *Casualty reclaimed.* One significant outcome was that
Mark made good. From his first imprisonment at Rome, Paul
wrote of Mark as a fellow worker (Phile. 24) and a comfort to
him (Col. 4:10-11). To earn such commendation, Mark must
have spent some time along the way faithfully serving with
Paul. In his last recorded epistle, written from a Roman dun-
geon, Paul asked that Mark be sent to him "because he is
helpful to me in my ministry" (2 Tim. 4:11, NIV). In his final
days Paul wanted one whom he had rejected in his earlier
years.

The deputy president of The Navigators, LeRoy Eims, tells
about a recruit, Johnny, joining his evangelistic team in Eims'
first year in Christian service. Things went well for several
months as Johnny served faithfully and enthusiastically. Then
one weekend Johnny f iled to arrive for team witnessing on
the Iowa State University campus. For no apparent reason, he
had simply decided not to come. The following Monday Eims
informed Johnny that he was no longer on the team because he
had broken one of the standards of the group. Johnny took it
hard.

Two weeks later Eims received a letter from Johnny, thank-
ing him for making it mean something to be part of the team,
then listing thirteen reasons why he should be reaccepted.
Eims immediately welcomed him back. Johnny became one of
the most productive men on the team. In later years he served
the Lord on two continents. Says Eims, "As I look back over a
twenty-year perspective, I know I would handle the situation

differently today. I would be quicker to show the tenderness and gentleness of Christ" (*Be the Leader You Were Meant to Be,* Victor Books, 1975, pp. 62-63). Perhaps as Paul and Barnabas looked back on the incident that led to their break-up, they both might have wished they had handled it differently.

Who was right in that controversy? In one sense both were wrong because of their stubbornness and sharpness. But in another sense, both were right, for it took the combination of Paul's toughness and Barnabas' tenderness to jolt Mark to full repentance and new resolve. Paul's rigidity made Mark aware of the seriousness of his failure and became a constant spur to constancy. Barnabas' gentle support provided the atmosphere for his reclamation.

Mark traveled widely preaching the Gospel. Tradition says he evangelized in Egypt and North Africa. St. Mark's Square in Venice is named for him. And the same Mark gave us the Gospel of the perfect Servant, the Lord Jesus Christ. The man who failed at first as a servant wrote about the unfailing supreme Servant in the second book of the New Testament. Through divine providence, this parting between two outstanding leaders contributed to this great blessing to the church.

# 6.
# *Corinthian Cliques*

In a parable titled "A Brawling Bride," Karen B. Mains describes a suspenseful moment in a wedding ceremony. With the handsome bridegroom and attendants in place at the front of the altar, and the sound of the organ signaling the bridal march, everyone rises to get a glimpse of the lovely bride. A horrible gasp bursts from the guests. The bride is limping. Her leg seems twisted. Her gown is torn and muddied. Bruises show on her bare arms. Her nose is bloody. Her eye is purple and swollen. Her hair is mussed. Does not this immaculate Prince who has kept Himself faithful to His bride deserve better than this? His bride, the church, has been fighting again! (*The Key to a Loving Heart,* David C. Cook, 1979, pp. 143–144)

Consider these actual situations:

In a Canadian church that had no middle aisle, but rather a divider down the center of the pews, two families at loggerheads managed always to sit one on one side and one on the other.

In a Pennsylvania church two services were held at the same time each Sunday morning. Some twenty people met in the main auditorium with the pastor who had been voted out but who refused to leave, continuing to control the money as treasurer. Downstairs over eighty folk were led in worship by a returned missionary who at their invitation was acting as pastor till the deposed minister left. Sometimes a state trooper parked outside to ensure order.

An amusing news story from Wales told of a feud in a church looking for a new pastor. It read: "Yesterday the two opposition groups both sent ministers to the pulpit. Both spoke simultaneously, each trying to shout above the other. Both called for hymns, and the congregation sang two—each side trying to drown out the other. Then the groups began shouting at each other. Bibles were raised in anger. The Sunday morning service turned into a bedlam. Through it all, the two preachers continued trying to outshout each other with their sermons.

"Eventually a deacon called a policeman. Two came in and began shouting for the congregation to be quiet. They advised the forty persons in the church to return home. The rivals filed out, still arguing. Last night one of the group called a 'let's-be-friends' meeting. It broke up in argument."

The item was headlined, "Hallelujah! Two Jacks in One Pulpit." It could have been bannered, "Two Factions in One Fellowship."

In the Corinthian fellowship there were four factions. Paul began his letter to this church, "Now I beseech you, brethren, by the name of our Lord Jesus Christ, that ye all speak the same thing, and that there be no divisions among you; but that ye be perfectly joined together in the same mind and in the same judgment" (1 Cor. 1:10).

The next verse speaks of "quarreling" (NASB), a word elsewhere translated "strife" (Gal. 5:20), and a much harsher word than the "divisions" of 1 Corinthians 1:10. A division or schism may form without creating nasty feelings, but a contentious quarrel suggests expression of animosity. The church was split into four factions.

Similar situations have recurred repeatedly through the centuries. Someone penned this parody of "Win Them One by One."

You split the one next to you,
And I'll split the one next to me;
In no time at all,
We'll split them all,
So split them, split them, one by one.

## Informants

Paul wrote to the Corinthians about five years after starting the church there. Word had reached him in Ephesus concerning several problems in the Corinthian church. He responded with this letter which has been called the outstanding textbook on pastoral theology. A major problem was division in the church body, reported by a source Paul was careful to mention.

Too often information is passed along in this fashion, "Pastor, did you know that so-and-so is doing this—but don't let him know I told you." Or an anonymous letter arrives, "Dear Deacon, Mr. X is a hypocrite. I hope you discipline him. From a faithful follower in Christ."

One pastor on receiving a phone call with such information replies, "I'll be glad to take that up with the party if I can use your name." Almost always the caller expresses horror at the thought of personal implication. But not Paul's informants. Chloe and her household were quite willing to speak up and be identified (1 Cor. 1:11).

The verb translated *hath been declared* means "made evident or clear." Paul writes what he knows to be true. And the information came to him personally. He is not reacting to a rumor, nor was he relying on a single witness.

A story is told of a big, faithful German shepherd dog on a pioneer farm. One day, as the farmer was returning from the field in late afternoon, he saw the dog apparently attacking his frightened, four-year-old. The farmer took out his gun, standard equipment on the frontier, and there in front of the house, shot the dog. Then, as the child sobbed out his story, the farmer moved the dog's dead body to find a large, dead rattlesnake which the dog had killed. The snake, not the child, had been the object of the dog's attack. It's important always to get our facts straight.

## Cliques

In a Canadian church with a succession of four pastors in eleven years, some old-timers often expressed a preference for Pastor A. "He knew how to get along with people," they reminisced. Others claimed Pastor B as their favorite, "What a communicator!" Still others lauded Pastor C, saying, "He was such a great visitor." Finally, another group favored the current Pastor D, because "he's such an able administrator."

Believers were similarly divided at Corinth. They formed cliques around four names. Some lined up behind Paul, saying, "I follow Paul." Others bragged, "I support Apollos." Others claimed, "I like Peter." The superspiritual—or genuinely wise—declared, "I [am] of Christ" (1 Cor. 1:12).

Experts in interpersonal relationships tell us that when people line up consistently on one side and others on the opposite, such differences can be destructive. But if Mr. A finds himself voting with Mr. B on some issues, though occasionally against him on others, polarization of positions is avoided. But at Corinth the same people lined up inflexibly, always behind the same leader, resulting in party spirit and party strife.

● *The Paul party.* Since Paul was the founder of the church, many believers would make him preeminent, especially those converted under his ministry. Proud of their association with him, they looked on successors as rivals. When later preachers came, his supporters quickly noted differences from Paul's style and enlarged the halo around the apostle's head. Traditionalists to the core, they probably lamented the passing of "the good old days." The status quo was enshrined.

When a New England pastor moved to another church after a twenty-year ministry, his former parishioners still clung to him, calling him back to officiate at weddings and funerals, much to the distress of the new pastor. The district superintendent, getting wind of the situation, reminded the church that their former pastor had indeed moved to a different congregation, and official ties should be broken. This meant the new, young pastor should be invited to officiate at all such functions. Happily, the church took the advice.

• *The Apollos party.* Apollos, who came to Corinth after Paul left, was an eloquent preacher and "mighty in the Scriptures" (Acts 18:24). Perhaps with his brilliance and Alexandrian background, he tried to relate Christianity to philosophy. "He can certainly sway an audience," some marveled. Apollos did not encourage this excessive admiration. In fact, his unwillingness to widen this split at Corinth may have delayed his return (1 Cor. 16:19).

But some people who might not have been too happy with Paul switched loyalty to Apollos. Sometimes in modern church situations, folks disgruntled with a former pastor come out of the woodwork to rally around a new man.

• *The Peter party.* Though Cephas (Peter) may not have even yet visited Corinth, he had a loyal following there. Known as the apostle to the Jews, he would attract those who believed in observing the Mosaic Law. Well known as number one of the twelve apostles, in the thinking of many he would rank far ahead of the Johnny-come-latelies Paul and Apollos.

• *The Christ party.* The fourth faction said, "We follow no human leader. And we go back farther than even Peter. We go back to Christ." It's remotely possible that some had seen Christ in the flesh. Possibly a few based their creed on some portion of His teaching which had somehow fallen into their hands.

At any rate, this group by their affirmation of Christ may have proudly implied that all others did not belong to Christ as they did, relegating such believers to a second-class status.

Paul had no objection to legitimate honors given to other preachers. But he knew that exalting any man unduly would erect a fence around him and create an exclusiveness that dishonored the name of Christ, with a theme song like this:

Believe as I believe, no more, no less;
That I am right, and no one else, confess;

**79**

Feel as I feel, think only as I think;
Eat what I eat, and drink but what I drink;
Look as I look, do always as I do;
And then, and only then, I'll fellowship with you.

• *Through the centuries.* The Corinthian cliques have had their successors down through the centuries. Some groups claim to preach the simple Gospel; others, the Gospel with the full complement of points. Some idealize a system of theology; others exult in liturgy and ritual; still others hold high "the Bible and the Bible alone." Doubtless each has a legitimate point. But ever present lurks the danger of looking down on others whose emphasis varies from ours.

Some jokesters tell about the three churches situated at the same downtown intersection. One congregation could be heard singing, "Will there be any stars in my crown?" followed by the second's, "No, not one," and the third's triumphant, "Oh, that will be glory for me."

A group of theologians were discussing predestination and free will. When the argument became heated, the dissidents split into two groups. One man, unable to make up his mind which group to join, slipped into the predestination crowd. Challenged as to why he was there, he said, "I came of my own free will." The group retorted, "Free will? You can't join us!" He retreated to the opposing group and met the same challenge. "I was sent here," he answered honestly. "Get out!" they stormed. "You can't join us unless you come of your own free will." And the confused Christian was out in the cold.

Charles Wesley wrote some of his hymns to promote his brother John's doctrine of entire sanctification. The second verse of his "Love Divine, All Loves Excelling" asks God to "take away our bent to sinning." This was too much for Calvinist Augustus Toplady. In a magazine of which he was editor, Toplady wrote an article in refutation, detailing a picture of man's potential for sinning. He arrived at the mathematical conclusion that a man of eighty is guilty of many millions of sins, a debt he can never hope to pay but for which he need not despair because of the sufficiency of Christ. He closed the article with an original poem, "A Living and Dying Prayer for the Holiest Believer in the World." This poem, now one of the most beloved hymns of all times, and known under the title, "Rock of Ages," was born out of party spirit (Frederick John Gilman, *The Evolution of the English Hymn,* Macmillan, 1927, pp. 223–225).

A divisive issue among evangelicals in Dwight Moody's day was eschatology, the doctrine of the future. Postmillenarian teaching was giving way to premillenarian interpretation. In the 1890s, when the premillenialists began to dispute among themselves, Moody advised them, "Don't criticize if our watches don't agree about the time we know He is coming." Moody extended invitations to post- as well as premillenarians to speak in his conferences, saying, "We will not have division."

Paul rebuked the jealousy and division occasioned by human exaltation. Had a fundamental doctrine been the issue, Paul would have taken sides. None of the cliques seemingly held heretical views. The error on the Resurrection, treated in 1 Corinthians 15, may have been a general misconception held by some in all groups.

Divisions crop up today in many areas of church life. In preparation for this book, I wrote several minister-friends to ask what episode had caused the greatest friction during their pastorates. Answers ranged from overambitious staff members and denominational loyalty on the one hand, to relocation projects, bank loans, and failure to go through proper channels for program approval on the other hand. One church which had voted unanimously on a $130,000 building program found itself at strong disagreement over a $35 purchase of used choir robes. One pastor could recall a serious quarrel, but couldn't remember what about. Burton C. Murdock, New York State director for Conservative Baptists, said, "From my perspective, church conflict has reached epidemic proportions." One church, strongly polarized over whether or not to support foreign missions, took two special offerings a year, one at Christmas for the current fund and the other at Easter for missions overseas, but found that each offering was boycotted by the opposition. A new pastor suggested that both offerings should be divided equally between the work at home and missions overseas. The happy result was that both offerings tripled and, more importantly, the "either-or" attitude disappeared.

As long as our knowledge is imperfect and our preferences varied, Christians will disagree on doctrinal emphases, organizational structures, liturgical matters, business procedures, and practical approaches, thus perpetuating ecclesiastical divisions. Such proliferation may contribute to the vigor and devoutness of Christianity as a whole. Paul does not rebuke the existence of denominations fostered by conscientious conviction, but does regret fragments wrenched from the whole body by contentious, conceited people.

Too often church fights start with substantive issues, then develop into interpersonal battles, so that to separate the two is difficult. Speed Leas and Paul Kittlaus comment, "A sign of conflict poorly managed can be seen when the antagonists do battle, not in terms of the current issue, but in terms of the historic commitments to 'our side.' Instead of asking the question, Which side of the issue should I be on this time? the question gets asked, Which way is my team going? I'll go with them right or wrong" (*Church Fights*, Westminster Press, 1937, p. 37).

## Correctives

Good-natured banter is harmless, like the remark of one pastor with a twinkle in his eye to a pastor of a different denomination: "Of course, we both do God's work, you in your way, and I in His." Diversity need not lead to division. Paul had some correctives for feuding factions that develop because of the exaltation of human personality.

●  *One team.* Paul asked three questions in 1 Corinthians 1:13. First, "Is Christ divided?" The verb *divided* derives from a noun meaning "part." Has Christ been broken into parts so that four cliques each has a quarter of Him? No group has a corner on a part of Christ, nor does any faction have all of Him exclusively for itself. All of Christ is for every believer individually and for every group of believers. Christ cannot be divided into bits and pieces.

Each segment of Christians should try to learn from the emphases of other groups instead of haughtily withdrawing to its own corner. Remember the six blind men who were asked to describe an elephant after touching it? The one who touched its leg compared it to a tree. The one who touched its side, a wall. Its ear was likened to a fan, its trunk to a snake, its tusk to a spear, and its tail to a rope. Each man needed the input of the others to get a complete picture.

Truth is multifaceted. The Holy Spirit used four men, Matthew, Mark, Luke, and John, to give us a balanced picture of Jesus Christ as King, Servant, Man, and God. None of the Gospels is more faithful to Christ than the others. A saintly bishop once said, "For the last thirty years I have been trying to see the features of Jesus Christ in every Christian man who differs from me." How foolish to build a wall around some section of truth and fail to see truth in other believing groups.

The second question Paul asked: "Was Paul crucified for you?" Did any of those preachers lauded by the Corinthians die on a cross to make atonement for sin? Disgust and sorrow must have choked Paul to think any clique at Corinth would bestow on any human the honor and trust due exclusively to the eternal Saviour who gave Himself for them.

The third question from Paul: "Were ye baptized in the name of Paul?" Baptism is administered in the name of Jesus Christ, which means identification with and submission to that divine Person. None of the Corinthians had been baptized in the name of Paul, Apollos, or Peter.

Someone has suggested we should turn our denominational nouns into adjectives. Instead of saying, "I am a Baptist, Methodist, Calvinist, Arminian, Charismatic, Fundamentalist, etc.," we should designate ourselves as Baptist Christians, Methodist Christians," and so forth, to accent our Christian oneness. After meeting genuine believers of another persuasion, rather than commenting, "He baptizes by immersion," or "He speaks in tongues," we would say, "He's a Christian brother (or sister); we have a claim on each other."

A white-haired man stood before a gallery painting of Christ. Face aglow, he murmured, "Bless Him; I love Him." A stranger overheard and said, "Brother, I love Him too," and clasped the old man's hand. A third man caught the word and joining his hand said, "I love Him too." Before the picture stood a group of people, hand clasped to hand, strangers but united in one Lord. They discovered they belonged to different denominations, but they belonged primarily to Christ. Putting Christ before human leaders will help fulfill Paul's wish "that there should be no schism in the body" (1 Cor. 12:25).

● *Vanity of human wisdom.* Just as we cheer a favorite athletic team, ancient Greeks supported their favorite philosophers in a sort of fan club. This wordly practice had crept into the Corinthian church so that people lined up behind their favorite wisdom dispenser: the erudite Paul, the eloquent Apollos, or the chief disciple Peter. Because the Corinthians gave inordinate prominence to human wisdom, Paul devoted considerable space to contrasting true and false wisdom (1 Cor. 1:14–4:7).

He pointed out that man never found God through his own wisdom. The message of reconciliation through Calvary's cross sounded ridiculous to the Greeks and scandalous to the Jews. Yet the "foolishness" of preaching the Cross brought the power of God into the lives of believing Corinthians so they overcame all sorts of wickedness. Paul's preaching was deliberately "without enticing words of man's wisdom" (2:4). Divine truth could never come through the brilliance of the natural man but only by the revelation of God and illumination of the Holy Spirit.

● *Men of clay.* Paul pointed up the folly of making heroes out of humans who are but servants of God. If the Corinthians had recognized these leaders as the messenger boys they were, parties would not have been formed to foolishly pit personality versus personality.

Paul, Apollos, and Peter were instruments in God's hand, recipients of God's gifts, performing service that was ineffective apart from empowerment by God. Each one could do only a part of God's work. Paul "planted" and Apollos "watered" the seed of God's Word, and God gave the increase (1 Cor. 3:6). Why exalt fallible men? Without the divine touch, some of our best service can be likened to the bungling of a child trying to help her mother:

The baby helped shell beans today,
Saved the waste, threw the good away.
I've thought how patient God must be,
When I help Him like she helps me.

A man visiting the countryside near Edinburgh, Scotland took pictures of the fences bordering the farm properties. One print showed his wife standing beside one of the fences. A few months later he took his children to Scotland to show them the same fences, but they could not be seen. A visitor explained, "You must have been here in the spring; now it's harvesttime and the grain is grown so high it blocks out the fences."

Instead of comparing their leaders, the Corinthians should have regarded them as complementary, rejoicing, "How blessed we are to have had all three and the benefit of all their gifts." The spiritual harvest should have obliterated their differences. Pastors today show wisdom in inviting guest pastors, evangelists, and Bible teachers so church members may enjoy the well-rounded ministry which a variety of leaders can provide.

As servants of God, Paul, Apollos, and Peter were responsible to Him and someday answerable to Him. By frivolously approving or rejecting God's ambassadors, the Corinthians officiously usurped a prerogative of God. So Paul wrote, "Judge nothing before the time, until the Lord come . . . and then shall every man have praise of God" (1 Cor. 4:5). Warning against judging does not apply to doctrinal heresy, immoral behavior, or schismatic action. The prohibition applies to secondary matters which sadly separate brothers in Christ.

Paul put his finger on the root cause of the Corinthian cliques: pride. Self-conceit lurks in the background of such partisanship. Vernon Grounds observed, "They had done essentially the same thing which a little boy does when he identifies himself with his father. As far as that boy is concerned, he and his father are emotionally one. And, consequently, the boy resents any criticism of his father; criticism of his father is construed as criticism of the boy, who has identified himself with his father" ("Christian Love and Church Problems" in *National Voice of Conservative Baptists,* Jan. 1953, p. 4). This spirit of rivalry—"My man is better than your man"—catered to their vanity. Instead of one for another, it became one against another, creating a four-way split. So Paul warned "that no one of you be puffed up for one against another" (1 Cor. 4:6).

Party faction was so serious at Corinth that Paul devoted more space to this problem than to any other in his first epistle to the church there. Perhaps the divisive spirit accentuated other problems, such as saint going to law against saint (chap. 6), the question of eating or abstaining from meat (chaps. 8–10), and unkindness at the Lord's table (11:17-22).

A year later Paul mentioned at the end of his second letter to Corinth his concern that his next visit might encounter "debates, envyings, wraths, strifes, backbitings, whisperings, swellings, tumults" (2 Cor. 12:20). It led to his closing plea, "Be of one mind, live in peace; and the God of love and peace shall be with you." Then he exhorted them to "greet one another with an holy kiss," a difficult act unless they had made peace with each other (13:11-12).

At the final rehearsal for the coronation of Queen Elizabeth II, a tension-releasing incident occurred just after the orchestra had sounded the final strains. The dignified archbishop stood erect by the altar, and nearby in ranks stood officers of state. A spine-tingling fanfare of trumpets burst out, signalling the queen's imminent entrance. But instead, four charwomen trotted in. Pushing four carpet sweepers, they nonchalantly proceeded to circle the throne, painstakingly seeking stray feathers and fuzz which had floated onto the golden carpet!

These maids had their place. Their lowly service was needed to preclude a sovereign's or statesman's sneeze! But no one would ever contemplate elevating these maids to a position of importance around whose leadership followers would rally in loyal support. It was the Queen who was to be honored.

Rather than exalt any human leader, whether Paul, Apollos, or Peter, the church must live as it sings:

All hail the power of Jesus' name,
Let angels prostrate fall,
Bring forth the royal diadem
And crown Him Lord of all.

# 7.
# When Brothers Offend

Lawyers Lynn R. Buzzard and Laurence Eck estimate that in one medium-size metropolitan area, 8,000 cases each year involve persons on both sides of legal disputes who call themselves Christians—with legal fees reaching perhaps $12 million (*Tell It to the Church*, David C. Cook, 1982, p. 25).

Is this the way Christian people are supposed to settle their differences?

During the regular midweek choir practice, Joe, a talented tenor, snapped at Chuck, the choir director. His remarks were not only cutting but uncalled for and unnecessarily personal. Joe thought he saw hurt in Chuck's face, but didn't see how he could take it seriously. Feeling a momentary impulse to apologize, he quickly brushed it aside. On Saturday evening Joe was going over his solo part for the choir special next morning when he suddenly recalled those unkind words spouted at Chuck. Should he do anything about the incident?

Though the church is one spiritual family, joined together as the body of Christ, sometimes brothers become unbrotherly, resulting in strained situations or broken relationships. Our Lord spoke several times about brothers at odds with each other. What comes through our Lord's teaching loud and clear is that it is sin for brothers to continue in an alienated state.

89

Jesus instructs both the offending, guilty party and the offended, innocent party to seek reconciliation. God holds both parties responsible for any continuing rift. In the above case, both offender Joe and innocent Chuck have definite responsibilities.

## The Duty of the Offender

In the Sermon on the Mount, Jesus said, "If you are offering your gift at the altar and there remember that your brother has something against you, leave your gift there in front of the altar. First go and be reconciled to your brother; then come and offer your gift" (Matt. 5:23-24, NIV).

Here's the biblical picture. A worshiper brings a lamb to the outer court of the temple to wait his turn for the officiating priest to receive the animal and sacrifice it in the inner court. In these moments only the most pressing matter would justify the withdrawal of the worshiper before offering the lamb. But in the holy hush he suddenly recalls that recently he offended a brother. Jesus teaches that he should forgo worship and make it right with his brother.

Jesus is not urging a habitual introspection at our worship services, nor is He suggesting that we postpone reconciliation till the next Communion service. The point is that if we have delayed making peace, we would do well to postpone even the most solemn worship to go on a peace mission. Apparently worship will not be wholehearted if we are at odds with a brother. To reconcile is better than sacrifice.

But it's not a choice between reconciliation and worship, but rather a matter of reconciliation in order to worship. Our adoration of God will be purer because of a restored relationship with our fellowman.

A lad was praying at Grandmother's knee, "If I should die before I wake, I pray . . . ." His voice trailed off.

"Go on, Johnny," Grandmother's voice prompted.

The little boy jumped to his feet. "Wait a minute," he exclaimed, then hurried down the stairs. In a few moments he was back to finish the prayer. When Grandmother questioned the little form tucked in bed, he exclaimed, "I began to think about what I was praying. I had set up my brother's wooden soldiers on their heads to see him get mad tomorrow morning. But if I should die before I wake, I didn't want him to find the mess, so I had to go and fix them."

Grandmother's comment was, "You did right. I imagine a good many prayers would be helped by stopping in the middle to undo a wrong."

The Church of England Communion service includes this caution, "Ye that . . . are in love and charity with your neighbors . . . draw near with faith."

Returning to the problem of Joe, the tenor soloist who suddenly recalled his insulting words to choir director Chuck, there was something that had to be done. So Joe got into his car, drove over to Chuck's home, blurted out a sincere apology, and asked forgiveness. Chuck admitted his simmering bitterness, and together they prayed. Both found their music ministry next morning an ecstatic delight.

## Forbearance

Was there anything that Chuck should have done, though he was the innocent, yelled-at, offended party? The New Testament has some definite rules for dealing with a brother who has wronged us.

• *Be slow to take offense.* How easy to feel someone has done us an injustice. One man called himself an "injustice collector," carrying around a trunk full of injustices. The unresolved anger felt against a brother becomes an "emotional scab" which we pick at until poison infects our relationship with that brother, our spiritual health, and possibly our physical welfare.

A pastor, asked the secret for happy marriages, replied, "Five bears—bear and forbear." The shrewd Ben Franklin advised, "Write injuries in dust, benefits in marble." Paul wrote that we should be "forbearing one another in love" (Eph. 4:2). We can overlook many slights and even indignities by the grace of Christ. Perhaps a recognition of others' personal stresses, business crises, or spiritual battles will help us sympathize and more readily forgive.

Forbearance with our brothers rules out scorekeeping of wrongs suffered, for love "keeps no record of wrongs" (1 Cor. 13:5, NIV). Nor does it make trophies out of hurt feelings, polishing and displaying them by reliving the hurts. Loving forbearance makes it possible to shrug off nasty things and not count them offenses. Perhaps some of us need to pray for a thick skin as well as a tender heart.

In her book *The Hiding Place,* Corrie ten Boom describes a reunion after a separation from her sister Betsie in a Nazi concentration camp. Corrie could see that her sister's face was swollen. Corrie, asking if a guard had beaten her, was amazed at Betsie's answer. "I felt so sorry for that man." What loving forbearance!

A brother was cheated of some inheritance money when his oldest sister passed away. The two surviving younger sisters had borrowed substantial sums from the deceased through the years which they never did pay back, and thus owed her estate. Acting as though they had never borrowed any money (for no documents had been signed) the two sisters inherited an equal amount with the brother, though his share should have been much more. By putting peace above money, the brother nobly overlooked the injustice, maintaining a friendly relationship with his two sisters the rest of their lives.

A widely used church covenant has members promising each other "to be slow to take offense, but always ready for reconciliation, and mindful of the rules of our Saviour, to secure it without delay." What are the Saviour's rules?

## Go to Your Brother

If the offense is serious enough to need righting, go to the offender and ask him to correct the wrong. This is Jesus' counsel: "If thy brother shall trespass against thee, go and tell him his fault between thee and him" (Matt. 18:15). Though we might be able to overlook an offense, some offenders need to be confronted for their own spiritual correction and maturity.

• *Do it quickly.* "Go and tell" is literally "Go, tell." Go right away. As we saw earlier, reconciliation takes precedence over worship. Making things right with your brother is important enough to make you hurry away from a scheduled devotional exercise.

Delay lets the injury fester. On a stone block built into a wall of Quebec City post office is carved the picture of a dog gnawing a bone. Originally placed over the door of a murdered man's house, the picture and accompanying words threaten revenge on nameless assailants:

I am a dog that gnaws his bone,
I crouch and gnaw it all alone;
The time will come, which is not yet,
When I'll bite him by whom I'm bit.

How harmful it is to mull over wrongs done us, "gnawing bones" of bitterness, polluting our souls. And the unrighted wrong continues to handicap our life until it is properly removed. It is our duty to get it off our chest.

A girl said, "Ten years ago my mother and uncle had a bitter fight and they stopped seeing each other. My mother missed him greatly. And I'm sure my uncle missed her too, for as brother and sister they had been like two peas in a pod. Recently when my mother became ill, my uncle heard of it and came to visit with a bouquet of flowers. Now they are the best of friends again." How sad for relatives to miss years of good times through alienation. Paul wrote, "Let not the sun go down upon your wrath" (Eph. 4:26). The longer the wound rankles, the more easily it will become a root of bitterness growing "up to cause trouble and defile many" (Heb. 12:15, NIV).

• *Each should take the initiative.* How easy for brothers at odds to reason that the other should make the first move. The offender reasons, "He deserves what he got. If it was so bad, he'll let me know and then I'll make things right." The offended one thinks, "He did the wrong. It wouldn't do any good for me to talk with him. I'd rather stay away from his kind. Let him come to me and apologize." Both sets of logic err. As previously cited, Jesus said in the Sermon on the Mount that the offender (who recalled that a brother had something against him) was to seek that brother out (Matt. 5:23-24). Jesus also said, as mentioned, that the offended one (who had something against his brother) should seek out the offender (Matt. 18:15). In other words, both offender and offended are responsible for making a move toward reconciliation. Both are under obligation to seek out the other. Brothers at odds, each on his way to find the other, should run into each other half-way.

Again, going back to the unkind remarks Joe made to Chuck, not only was Joe responsible for going to Chuck to make amends, but Chuck, because of his simmering resentment, should have driven over to Joe's home to tell him his fault privately. According to Christ's teaching, Chuck was as obligated as Joe to take the initial step.

• *Try to settle the case privately.* Jesus said, "Tell him his fault between thee and him alone" (Matt. 18:15). Try to meet the person face-to-face. If you are separated by hundreds of miles, urgency may require the use of the phone, which otherwise is a cop-out. If all alone when confronted, a brother may more readily acknowledge his fault than if approached by even a committee of two or three. If settled, the incident need never be known outside the circle of the two brothers. Dirty linen should not be needlessly washed in public view. So, before a matter gets on the official agenda of some board, far better to settle it privately. Outsiders who wish to rush in with advice should heed the warning of Proverbs 26:17, "He who meddles in a quarrel not his own is like one who takes a passing dog by the ears" (RSV).

• *Don't triangulate.* When X holds a grudge against Y, and tells Z about it, X may get some relief from unloading, and Z may feel honored to have been the confidant of X. Sometimes a troubled person needs the advice of another to gain balance on a problem, but too often divulgence of the matter only perpetuates an unresolved conflict. The process of involving a third party in a gossiping context is called triangulating. Sowing discord among the brethren is something God hates (Prov. 6:19).

When a member began to complain to a friend about the way the adult Bible school teacher was giving the lesson, the friend wisely advised, "Why don't you go tell him how you feel and quit your complaining? Don't tell others; tell him."

Minor disagreements or misunderstandings can so easily escalate into massive conflicts, including personal attacks and choosing of sides. The refusal to triangulate can help avoid such tragedies.

● *Confront in love and in the spirit of reconciliation.* Counselors tell us of two wrong, harmful ways to handle anger, and a third, healing way. To bottle up anger internally is to strain both our emotional and physical systems. On the other extreme, to vent anger unrestrainedly is to destroy a relationship. So what do we do?

Realistically admit, "I am getting angry. I don't want to be angry, so please help me with this anger."

To convince a person that he has done wrong may be a difficult and delicate assignment. Argument may develop. Self-control, humility, and love are the most convincing "arguments" the offended can have. In reality, the health of the Christian body is at stake.

A widely known Bible teacher holding meetings in California made a sneering remark about a denomination which he believed taught wrong doctrine in secondary matters. Afterward a preacher in that denomination sought an interview with the Bible teacher and stated his grievance. The teacher quickly apologized and to make amends he asked the minister to invite several fellow ministers of that denomination to be his guests at a luncheon. At the table the offender began, "We know we have certain doctrinal differences, but during lunch today let's discuss only those points on which we agree. First, do we agree that Jesus Christ is God?" There was unanimous assent. They began to talk about what the Lord Jesus meant to them.

As the meal progressed, tension relaxed and a deepening fellowship followed. The Bible teacher, of course, apologized for his improper remark. Parting, they promised to pray for each other. Someone wrote,

> I was angry with my friend,
> I told my wrath, my wrath did end.

Don't go in the spirit of hostility, lambasting your brother in no uncertain terms for sinning against you and disobeying the Bible. Don't go in the spirit of superiority because you condescended to take the initiative. Don't go with the goal of winning a contest or getting even. But go already having forgiven him in your heart and with the single objective of restoring peace.

● *You may "gain your brother."* The alleged offense may have some logical explanation, or not be as bad as it seemed before discussion. The confrontation may bring new significant facts to light. But if the injury proves real and hurtful, and your brother agrees he was wrong, and asks forgiveness, then "thou has gained thy brother" (Matt. 18:15).

Even if a brother doesn't admit his fault, you still have the satisfaction of having tried to discover all the facts, of openness to your brother's viewpoint, of an honest attempt to effect reconciliation, and of obedience to a command of Jesus. To go is not an option. To go to an offending brother is as much a command as to go into all the world and proclaim the Gospel.

But having failed a reconciliation, what would be your next step?

## Enlist the Help of Other Brothers
If a private, personal approach proves fruitless, the next step is clear. Jesus said, "But if he will not hear thee, then take with thee one or two more, that in the mouth of two or three witnesses every word may be established" (v. 16). The issue now becomes semiprivate. The presence of a third party

serves several useful purposes, such as mellowing the conflict, opening avenues of communication, interpreting the issues, inhibiting rash statements, and establishing trust.

The added number may reinforce to the erring brother the seriousness of his offense and the necessity of making things right. Added counselors provide added wisdom. Most congregations have some sensitive and seasoned saints who, as neither protagonists nor antagonists, can act objectively as referees. These arbitrators need not hold formal office in the church, but because of their tactful manner and wisdom of experience, they may be instruments of peace.

In a Texas church where an officer stopped attending worship services, and none of his fellow board members wanted to risk losing his friendship by confronting him, the pastor decided to take action himself. Visiting the man, the pastor suggested he needed to become more active or else resign his board position, or take another church position that didn't take so much time. All seemed to go smoothly, but the following day the pastor received several phone calls from people wanting to know why he asked this board member to resign. The board member and his family left the church because of the pastor. It took several months before the false rumors faded away. The pastor admitted that his mistake was in acting alone: "The situation could have been avoided if I'd insisted on at least one officer accompanying me. I should have waited till someone was willing."

Taking someone with you may win your brother. A woman cheated out of $50,000 by a business partner was counseled to forgive. Forgive the loss of $50,000? Deciding this was possible, and accompanied by her counselors, she visited her former partner and his wife, who had avoided her, as she had them, for over two years. Telling them she knew what they had done, she was now forgiving them. Her former partner broke down, confessed his sin, tearfully begged her forgiveness, and promised to repay the entire amount as able.

If this conference of informal judges cannot settle the matter because the erring party will not listen, apologize, or make restitution, the counselors will be witnesses before the church. The offender will not be able to change his story, deny his words, nor claim forgetfulness of statements made. The situation has reached a very serious stage at this point.

## Tell It to the Church

Jesus suggests a three-step process (Matt. 18:15-17) for a brother to follow when a fellow believer has offended him.

> First, go to your brother privately.
> If the matter is not resolved, then
> take one or two witnesses along with you.
> If still not resolved, tell it to the church.

One church covenant reads, "We will not bring to the church a complaint against any member for personal trespass or offense until we have taken the first and second steps pointed out by Christ, thus endeavoring to settle all private offenses without publicity."

● *Don't take it to court.* Suing has become a way of life for Americans. Twenty times as many lawyers practice in the U.S.A. as in Japan. America has over ten times as many civil complaints as many European nations. This practice has not escaped the Christian community. Churches are entangled in legal battles with other churches. Prominent Christian musicians and composers have brought suit against thirty Christian radio stations. Churches and denominational headquarters have gone to court over church property. A couple brought suit against the Southern Baptist Convention, the nation's largest Protestant group, alleging that the denomination's president violated its bylaws by refusing to permit nominations from the floor for an important committee.

By going to law Christians may be violating a very clear command of Scripture. Paul rebuked the Corinthians:

> If any of you has a dispute with another, dare he take it
> before the ungodly for judgment instead of before the

saints? Do you not know that the saints will judge the
world? And if you are to judge the world, are you not
competent to judge trivial cases? Do you not know that
we will judge angels? How much more the things of this
life! Therefore, if you have disputes about such matters,
appoint as judges even men of little account in the
church! I say this to shame you. Is it possible that there
is nobody among you wise enough to judge a dispute
between believers? But instead, one brother goes to law
against another—and this in front of unbelievers! (1 Cor.
6:1-6, NIV)

How amazing that a Christian destined to judge angels would
not let even an unimportant believer judge his grievance
against his brother. What a shame for Christians to go before
unbelievers to settle their differences. Paul goes on to say that
it would be preferable to allow yourself to be defrauded than to
haul another brother before a secular judge. "Why not rather
be wronged? Why not rather be cheated? Instead, you yourselves cheat and do wrong, and you do this to your brothers"
(vv. 7-8, NIV).

Granted, certain situations involve wrongs of such a nature
that they must be challenged in court. For example, a Christian wife badly abused by a husband (once a professing Christian but now excommunicated from the church) needs to go to
court for protection. But in many cases, suffering loss instead
of legal recourse would make an impact for the Gospel.

Christian belief and behavior are tailor-made for the restoration of broken relationships. The doctrines of reconciliation and
of forgiveness, and the graces of patience, long-suffering,
peacemaking, gentleness, and humility dovetail into the task of
conflict solving.

● *Bring it before the church.* When the matter comes before
the church, both brothers should be present and permitted to
present their cases. If the erring brother repents, he should
receive immediate forgiveness. Significantly, the next section
in Matthew 18, after dealing with brothers at odds, is a parable

in which Jesus teaches readiness to forgive oft-repeated offenses. Jesus, who commands honest, prompt confrontation
between brothers at odds, makes an equally strong case for
full, loving forgiveness (vv. 21-35).

When Moravian missionaries first went to the Eskimos,
they could not find a word in the Eskimos' language for "forgiveness." So they made one up. The long compound meant
literally "not-being-able-to-think-about-it-anymore." True forgiveness may not always completely remove a wound from the
memory, but it does transform the recollected grudge into
thanksgiving.

If a fellow believer is judged guilty by the congregation, and
he stubbornly refuses to right the wrong, he must be
disfellowshipped. Jesus' verdict is severe: "If he shall neglect
to hear the church, let him be unto thee as an heathen man
and a publican" (Matt. 18:17). Paul backs up Jesus' order:
"Warn a divisive person once, and then warn him a second
time. After that, have nothing to do with him" (Titus 3:10,
NIV).

● *The authority of the church.* The action of the church is
taken as the action of heaven. Matthew 18:18 says, "Whatsoever ye shall bind on earth shall be bound in heaven; and
whatsoever ye shall loose on earth shall be loosed in heaven."
Then a little later it adds, "For where two or three are gathered together in My name, there am I in the midst of them"
(v. 20). This verse all too often gives comfort to churches that
attract only a few to prayer meetings.

Ronald Kraybill says the context leaves no room for this
interpretation, but deals with relationships and misunderstandings. He adds, "Moreover, 'two or three gathered' is a phrase
familiar from Old Testament usage in the context of adjudicat-
ing disputes; it indicates an acceptable quorum of witnesses
(cf: Deut. 17:6; 19:15; Heb. 10:28; et al). Thus it is clear that
Jesus' words are intended for peacemakers. Where believers
gather to resolve disputes in His name, Christ is present
among them" (*Repairing the Breach,* Herald Press, 1980, p.
13). The church's decision, though not infallible, is to be re-

ceived as final and unappealable, the best the church could do.

The authors of *Tell It to the Church* suggest that it's not necessary for the whole church to hear the dispute: "The Corinthian passage (chapter 6) seems to suggest that the body appoint some individuals who are gifted and called to peace-making as reconcilers and mediators. The church in Matthew 18 and 1 Corinthians 6 should not be seen exclusively in terms of the local congregation, but in terms of the whole body" (p. 33). They point out that since many disputes involve more than one church fellowship, or individuals from different churches, and even denominations or parachurch organizations, it will be critical to assemble a judicial entity that will be able to deal with the larger body of Christ.

The Christian Conciliation Service, a recently formed arm of the Christian Legal Society, provides a network of evangelical lawyers as mediators or arbitrators in several metropolitan areas nationwide. CCS has developed some general procedures in the application of Christian conciliation for parties to follow when they have a dispute. The processes for conciliation are outlined in a chapter in *Tell It to the Church* (pp. 77–84). *Repairing the Breach* also has a chapter, "A Procedure for Mediating Inter-Personal Disputes" (pp. 60–71). Similar material is found in a concise manual, *Conquering Church Crises*, by Burton C. Murdock, New York State director of Conservative Baptists (P.O. Box 1415, Oneonta, NY 13820). The judges of disputes should include, along with lawyers, representatives of all strata of the church community, not only the influential but "even men of little account in the church!" (1 Cor. 6:4, NIV) Such Christian juries should prove a boon to an already overworked legal profession unable to handle its multitudinous and ever-expanding caseload.

A highly charged custody case resolved by the CCS pitted a natural mother against the adoptive parents. A twenty-three-year-old single girl who became pregnant refused an abortion. After pastoral counsel she decided to offer the baby for adoption. A fine Christian couple took the new infant boy into their home. Seven months later the girl decided she wanted her baby, but the adoptive parents, who had the law on their side because the legal waiting period had expired, did not wish to give the little lad up. With the case certainly headed for the courts, a Christian lawyer suggested that the girl and the parents submit the case to an arbitration council of believers and abide by its verdict. The principals agreed. Three well-qualified Christians were selected. After praying, hearing both sides, and deliberating, the panel awarded the baby to the adoptive parents. Of course, the girl was disappointed, but she accepted the decision, even demonstrating a fine Christian spirit by embracing the adoptive mother.

Paul's counsel to the Colossian church helps make Christian brotherhood a reality:

> Clothe yourselves with compassion, kindness, humility, gentleness, and patience. Bear with each other and forgive whatever grievances you may have against one another. Forgive as the Lord forgave you. And over all these virtues put on love, which binds them all together in perfect unity. Let the peace of Christ rule in your hearts, since as members of one body you were called to peace. And be thankful" (Col. 3:12-15, NIV).

# 8.

# Banishing
# in Order to Bless

Marian Guinn, longtime member of the Church of Christ in Collinsville, Oklahoma (pop. 2,200), had been treated kindly by this 125-member congregation. Several had helped her obtain her high school equivalency diploma by providing baby-sitting and car expense. They gave a party for her when she graduated from Tulsa Junior College a few years later.

In 1981, after hearing persistent reports that she was having an affair with the town mayor, elders met with her, prayed, and urged her to break off the relationship. The affair continued. In a letter dated September 21, 1981, the church leaders warned her that unless she publicly repented, they would take it before the church. Without denying any of the allegations, she insisted it was none of their business. On September 24, she wrote a letter of resignation, thus hoping to end the matter by removing herself from church jurisdiction.

But the church proceeded. On September 27, a letter was read to the congregation, asking members to speak to Miss Guinn about "the condition of her soul" and giving her until October 4 to repent. A day after the deadline, another letter went out listing some Scriptures they claimed she had violated, announcing the removal of her name from membership, and asking the members to pray for her and to exhort her. The letter was also forwarded to four close sister congregations in the immediate area.

Miss Guinn filed suit against the church and its three elders for invasion of her privacy, for highly offensive revelations which permanently injured her good name, and for severe emotional distress caused by their extreme and outrageous conduct. Telling the court that what she did was between God and herself, she claimed that the elders had no right to interfere in someone else's life.

The jury awarded her $205,000 actual damages plus another $185,000 punitive damages. Undaunted by the action of the Oklahoma jury, the church leaders insisted their method of church discipline stemmed from biblical instructions set forth in Matthew 18. It was their solemn duty to admonish the members of the congregation.

Naturally, the press gave it headline coverage, depicting the church as nosing into a person's private life. At this writing, the case is sitting in appeal in the Oklahoma Supreme Court and, because of the crucial church-state issues involved, will undoubtedly go to the U.S. Supreme Court.

Even before this case had gone to trial before the appellate courts, several similar cases of congregants suing churches were filed across the country.

## The Mandate to Exercise Discipline

Church discipline—judging people and exposing their shortcomings to public view—is a touchy matter. Since great damage has been caused in the name of church admonishment, should we relinquish the practice so as to avoid public censure and legal hassles?

Though not always easy for church leaders to determine when a believer deserves disfellowship, certain Bible texts give the basis for withdrawing association:

> If he refuses to listen even to the church, let him be to you as a Gentile and a tax-gatherer (Matt. 18:17, NASB).

Brethren, mark them which cause divisions and offenses contrary to the doctrine which ye have learned, and avoid them (Rom. 16:17).

You must not associate with anyone who calls himself a brother but is sexually immoral or greedy. . . . Are you not to judge those inside? (1 Cor. 5:11-12, NIV)

Keep aloof from every brother who leads an unruly life and not according to the tradition which you received from us (2 Thes. 3:6, NASB).

A man that is an heretic after the first and second admonition reject (Titus 3:10).

Note the words: *avoid; must not associate with; keep aloof; reject*. These words may be translated or paraphrased in the following ways: "steer clear of"; "expel"; "disassociate"; "have no dealings with"; "shun"; "withdraw companionship." Interestingly, the word *companion* is a combination of the two Latin words meaning "with" and "bread." A believer is not to break bread on a spiritual level with a person who has been disfellowshipped.

One mark of a healthy church is the exercise of discipline. The degree of discipline may differ from a mild rebuke to a short suspension to an act of excommunication. If a church has the right to admit to membership, logically it has the power to expel. Membership which authenticates fellowship is a correlative of excommunication which ends fellowship. Disciplining which accompanies membership in a local church is paralleled by discipline which separates from membership.

The *Heidelberg Catechism* of 1563 has this question:

How is the kingdom of heaven shut and opened by Christian discipline? The answer: In this way: Christ commanded that those who bear the Christian name in an unchristian way either in doctrine or in life should be given brotherly admonition. If they do not give up their errors or evil ways, notification is given to the church or to those ordained for this by the church. Then, if they do not change after this warning, they are forbidden to partake of the holy Sacraments and are thus excluded from the communion of the church and by God Himself from the kingdom of Christ. However, if they promise and show real amendment, they are received again as members of Christ and of the church.

Discipline preserves the integrity, witness, and essence of the church. It shows that the church is the church. When the charge is made that the church is acting outrageously in disciplining someone living in adultery, things are topsy-turvy. In reality, it is the church member-adulterer who is acting outrageously. And the church would be acting outrageously if it failed to exercise discipline. A few years ago, adulterous conduct, especially by a church member, would have been considered indecent. How ironic the current claim that a church is acting beyond the bounds of decency when it disciplines on the grounds of immoral behavior.

In addition, when government intrudes into the internal affairs of a church, it is interfering in the biblically mandated doctrine and duty of the church. Such meddling is unwarranted entanglement into the area of protection extended by the First Amendment, "Congress shall make no law respecting an establishment of religion or prohibiting the free exercise thereof." The church must be free to be countercultural and otherworldly. Otherwise it would be forced to mirror the morals of this world, and fail to be the salt of the earth. Church discipline is the business of the church, not the courts.

## Reasons for Avoidance

On what grounds should Christians withdraw fellowship from a fellow believer? Throughout church history three major reasons have been given: heresy, scandal, and schism.

● *Serious doctrinal error (heresy).* In an adult Bible school class, a member who had recently joined the church by letter from another church revealed that he did not believe in the literal, bodily resurrection of Jesus Christ. When kind and repeated attempts over a period of several months in both private confrontation and deacon committee meetings failed to convince him of the truth of this fundamental doctrine of the Christian faith, the church voted to erase his name from their membership list.

Jesus warned of false prophets (Matt. 7:15). Paul alerted the Ephesian elders "that after my departing shall grievous wolves enter in among you" (Acts 20:29). Peter foretold that "there shall be false teachers among you, who privily shall bring in damnable heresies, even denying the Lord that bought them" (2 Peter 2:1).

Though the peace of a church is an important matter, it is not to be peace at any price. The unity of the faith is broken by a person who with deliberation denies any essential doctrine. Jude exhorts his readers to "earnestly contend for the faith which was once delivered unto the saints" (Jude 3). Though not to be contentious, we are to be contenders for the truth. If a theologically liberal element begins to assert itself in a church, this group which is intruding, interfering, and interrupting by means of doctrinal aberrations should be invited to return to the once-for-all-delivered faith, or leave the fellowship of the church. Basic fundamental beliefs of Christianity include Christ's virgin birth, substitutionary atonement, bodily resurrection, His return, and the divine inspiration of Scripture. Anyone who denies any of these should seriously reconsider his right to remain within the membership of a Christian church.

When a theologically liberal group becomes strong, one of two courses of action has been followed by those loyal to conservative teaching. One was to remain and contend for the faith; the other was to pull out and start or join a theologically sound church. Writing to Timothy, Paul advised him to "withdraw" from those who did not hold to wholesome doctrine (1 Tim. 6:3-5). He named two men—Hymenaeus and Philetus—who corrupted truth by denying the doctrine of the future resurrection of the believer (2 Tim. 2:17-18).

When the Northern Baptist Convention seemed to permit

the appointment of missionaries who did not hold completely to the fundamentals of the faith, some churches broke away in the '30s to start the General Association of Regular Baptists. But many remained within the convention to try to reform from the inside. Sensing the futility of reform from within, still more churches broke away in the '40s to start the Conservative Baptist movement. Some that wanted reform chose to work within the framework of the old convention, and still do. Similarly in the '30s, because of liberalism, several churches chose to break with the Presbyterian Church USA. Many who chose to stay and fight from within did not withdraw till recent years, including such prestigious churches as Tenth Presbyterian in Philadelphia; First Presbyterian in Schenectady, New York; and Fourth Presbyterian in Bethesda, Maryland. This pattern has been repeated in many of the mainline denominations.

Since Romans 16:17 commands avoidance of those causing doctrinal error, the consensus of many scholars is that the culprits are proponents of antinomian libertinism. This heresy advocated a licentious lifestyle under the guise of Christian liberty. The gratification of fleshly lust brought into play the mercy of God since, where sin abounded, grace would much more abound. This false view downgraded holiness.

• *Scandal.* The *New York Daily News* carried this front page headline on April 23, 1986: "Church Sued by 'Sinners'— Pastor Rapped Lovers from Pulpit." The story told of a man and woman in the Mission Church in Carmel, New York, both with mates, who began to live with each other in 1983. The pastor called their conduct scandalous, and read a letter to the congregation explaining the situation. He quoted several Bible passages condemning adultery, and asked the congregation to pray for God to convict them of their sin and bring them to repentance. The couple then filed a civil lawsuit against the church for violation of confidentiality by revealing their living arrangement to the church's 275 members. The church's lawyer contended that the couple's living arrangement was already known to the town when the censure was issued.

Regardless of the disposition of the case just coming to trial at this writing, and apart from the merits of the procedure followed, the church was correct in exercising discipline. Said the pastor, "It was a real scandal. We felt we were doing what was biblical."

Good precedent for that church's action is found in the case of immorality mentioned in First Corinthians. A man in the Corinthian congregation was cohabiting with his stepmother, sins of adultery and incest forbidden by God and untolerated even by pagans. Almost as serious was the indifference of the church in the face of this flagrant iniquity which was bringing disgrace on the cause of Christ. Puffed up, they were bigheaded when they should have been brokenhearted.

So Paul directed that the man be removed from the church. The minimal meaning of his demand to "deliver such an one unto Satan" is the putting of the guilty man outside the bounds of church communion into the area dominated by the prince of this world (1 Cor. 5:5). Expulsion from Christian society would hopefully lead him to repent and live a life with the flesh crucified. Biblical standards plainly dictate that any unrepentant church member who indulges in flagrant immorality be put out of the fellowship (v. 13).

Disorderliness was also considered scandalous. For example, at Thessalonica some believers quit work because they thought the Second Coming of Christ was imminent. Their idleness led to gossiping, perhaps sponging on the church, and probably ridicule of the Gospel. Paul commands the Thessalonians to "withdraw yourselves from every brother that walketh disorderly" (2 Thes. 3:6). The man who does not work should not be fed, but rather avoided. "Note that man, and have no company with him" (vv. 11, 14).

Paul named several other sins for which fellowship should be withdrawn. Don't associate with anyone who calls himself a brother but is sexually immoral or greedy, an idolator or a slanderer, a drunkard or a swindler. With such a man do not even eat" (1 Cor. 5:11, NIV). Church history books indicate that in the seventeenth and eighteenth centuries discipline was much more widely practiced than in our day. People were disciplined for scandalous conduct involving amusements, dress, marriage choices, family life, drunkenness, and money matters.

Martin Luther once threatened to excommunicate a man who intended to sell a house for 400 gulden which he had purchased for 30. Luther suggested 150 gulden as reasonable. Though inflation had raised prices, Luther called the profit this man sought barefaced greed deserving of church discipline.

● *Schism.* After warning Titus to shun frivolous and fruitless questions that only stir up strife, Paul added, "A man that is an heretic after the first and second admonition reject" (Titus 3:9-10). Originally, a heretic was a person who caused divisions. From the verb *to choose,* heresy at first meant a party a man chose to join or a cause he elected to promote. Heresy later became private opinion or interpretation that opposed the teaching of the church. Paul probably used heretic here in its earlier significance to refer to a factious man fomenting quarrels and disputes. It should be noted, however, that erroneous opinions or false doctrines are ofttimes the cause of faction.

One church manual says refusal of a member to submit to church action constitutes factiousness. If he fails to heed a couple of admonitions, he will likely continue his divisive ways. So, as in baseball, three strikes means he's out.

Into a church which had always taught that every believer receives the baptism of the Holy Spirit at the moment of salvation came a couple dozen new members who believed that the baptism of the Spirit comes subsequent to salvation and is attested by the gift of tongues. This new teaching created unrest among some established members who began to feel they had not "arrived" spiritually. So the pastor and deacons met several times with the newcomers and asked them to refrain from spreading teaching which contradicted the official doctrine of the church. When the new group persisted in promoting their particular interpretation, almost to the point of splitting the congregation, the official board requested the resignations of the factious members.

If on the other hand, into a church which has always taught tongues as the sign of the Spirit's baptism comes a group of people who oppose that doctrine to the point of causing division, that new group should be asked to either desist from pushing their doctrinal viewpoint or leave the church.

## Procedures in Disfellowshipping

A man reportedly said, "I'm not the least bit afraid of thieves breaking into my house. I've got the place rigged so if I hear a burglar I touch a button that sends an electric current to explode the dynamite in my cellar. That will blow the burglar sky high!" We smile at such wild schemes, but church discipline can be almost as reckless and destructive.

● *Admonition comes first.* As we have seen in the previous chapter, a member guilty of heresy, scandal, or schism should usually be first approached privately by a concerned Christian. If unpersuaded from his errant ways, he should be visited by two or three church representatives. If still unrelenting, he should be asked to answer to the whole church.

● *The whole church acts.* The exercise of discipline belongs to the entire church. Anticipating the existence of the church and an irreconcilable brother, Jesus' injunction was "tell it unto the church" (Matt. 18:17). In an article, "Creative Church Discipline," Canadian pastor Michael E. Phillips suggests that when correcting wayward members, laxity and expulsion are not the only two options. Temporary suspension along with work assignments as spiritual therapy have been a frequent remedy. He says, "Since we began using temporary suspension rather than automatic expulsion, we have witnessed it work in almost every case. After a time of reflection, suspended members come back to us penitent and renewed, allowing us to guide them into their future ministries. Even when suspension failed to work, we knew that release was better than revenge" (*Leadership*, Fall Quarter, 1986, p. 50).

But some cases prove so serious that excommunication is the necessary recourse as in the case of the incestuous offender at Corinth. Paul instructed the church, "When ye are gathered together . . . put away from among yourselves that wicked person (1 Cor. 5:4, 13). Paul had just dealt in chapters 1–4 with church divisions at Corinth, knowing that to handle the matter of discipline a united church was essential.

If the accused offender should suddenly resign when a disciplinary action is about to be taken, a church weighing the factors may decide that under the circumstances no formal discipline is necessary. On the other hand, for biblical reasons (one of which is the spiritual benefit of the offender), a church may be reluctant to abandon the process entirely, and proceed to announce the verdict.

● *Banishment is firm.* Avoidance, as disfellowshipping is often called, establishes a relationship which convinces the disciplined brother in a firm yet loving way of the seriousness of his spiritual status. No backslapping camaraderie should deceive the offender into thinking the unpleasantness will blow over by itself. A radical change is required.

A decree of disfellowship must be maintained consistently by the congregation to make the action effective. Some Christians believe social friendships with the disobedient brother must be terminated. For example, a forty-eight-year-old potato farmer who challenged the authority of his church in a small Pennsylvania Amish sect was punished by excommunication and by shunning, a practice in which he was avoided by all church members, including his wife of thirteen years. She took their six children and moved out for nine months.

But it seems that disfellowship from a scriptural perspective should not bring about shunning but rather forbid conduct that would encourage an erring brother in further transgression. This is why John wrote that a false teacher should not be welcomed into a believer's home—"neither bid him God speed; for he that biddeth him God speed is partaker of his evil deeds" (2 John 10-11). Opposition to grievous sin must be plainly expressed.

● *But love does not stop.* To refuse hospitality to a false teacher is not to endorse unkindness or discourtesy. If a heretical teacher were hungry and shelterless, certainly John did not forbid the ordinary courtesies of life. Only in his official capacity is a false teacher not to receive help.

An article in *Christianity Today* (August 31, 1962) described a small group in Britain that practiced extreme separation from "nonbelievers" (those voted out of the fellowship). A seventy-three-year-old man reportedly had been compelled to leave his wife after thirty-seven years of happy married life. The distraught woman was labeled a "sinner" and the home "leprous." A press report told of a twenty-year-old who committed suicide after his parents were ordered by this same group to have no social contact with him. Because believers and "unbelievers" are not supposed to eat together, one account tells how this group hypocritically obeyed Scripture by make-believe sawing of a table in half so that it was technically two tables, though the halves were never parted.

But redemptive avoidance cannot mean such cutting off of all contact with offenders. After Paul commanded Christians not to keep company with disorderly idlers, he added, "Yet count him not as an enemy, but admonish him as a brother" (2 Thes. 3:15). How can one admonish a brother if he shuns him completely? In the hope of helping a brother be restored to God's way, normal civility, evident concern, and regular dialogue are to be maintained. Corporate and social activities of a spiritual nature are to be denied the unrepentant offender.

Neither does avoidance mean renunciation of family ties. Some Christians at Corinth concluded that the spiritual chasm between a believer and an unbelieving mate called for the breakup of the marriage, but Paul affirmed the opposite. Rather, the continuance of the relationship provides opportunity of witness to the unbeliever. Prudent avoidance discreetly uses natural, social, and marital association to remind the offender of his need and point him back to spiritual fellowship.

Disfellowshipping must walk a straight line that simultaneously affirms two truths: first, that a wayward believer has forfeited the privileges of fellowship by persisting in false and unrighteous ways; second, that he has an open invitation to return to fellowship upon repentance. Avoidance has been called "both excommunication and communication."

C. Peter Wagner points out that excommunication in the early church was rare. Though the Corinthian church was full of problems such as people embroiling in carnal divisions, getting intoxicated at the Lord's Supper, and abusing spiritual gifts, yet "Paul recommended excommunication for only one— a man living openly with his stepmother. Paul scolded the others but did not suggest that they had forfeited their right to church membership because they practiced such deeds. There are other passages where Paul sets forth high requirements for leaders, but not for ordinary members. Back then, as now, excommunication in the congregational structure or modality was rare" (*Leading Your Church to Growth*, p. 148).

## Purpose of Disfellowshipping
At least three purposes are served by withdrawal of fellowship, the last being the most important.

● *To refine the church.* When Paul rebuked the Corinthians for failure to deal with the case of immorality in their midst, he asked, "Don't you know how a little yeast can permeate the whole lump?" He then urged them to "clear out every bit of the old yeast that you may be a new unleavened bread!" (1 Cor. 5:6-7, PH)

Just as one sickly lamb may spread disease through an entire flock, or one little spark kindle a major fire, so one case of evil unchecked may spread spiritual disease all through a congregation. To stop the contagion before it infected the whole Corinthian body, the offender was to be expelled.

● *To dispel any false impression about the church.* When any church member is allowed to persist in heresy, scandal, or schism without any confrontation, the outside world receives a wrong concept of the church. Continuation of wrongdoing leads outsiders to think the church is unconcerned with righteousness. How easy for the world to conclude that "the church is full of hypocrites."

Since the reputation of the church depends on the lifestyle

of its members, discipline is required when any member goes astray, in order to send a signal to the community that the church stands strong and true for truth and purity.

● *To restore the erring brother.* Undoubtedly the major purpose of disfellowshipping is remedial, aiming at the repentance and restoration of the miscreant. Expulsion seems harsh, but is meant as a ministry. For if the sinning brother, whose life is warped and unhappy, can be brought back through withdrawal of fellowship, then chords that were broken will vibrate once more in harmony and happiness. Like earthly fathers, the Heavenly Father doesn't punish His children to torture them, but to correct them.

To show the purpose of banishment, Paul uses expressions such as "that they may learn not to blaspheme" (1 Tim. 1:20), "that he may be ashamed" (2 Thes. 3:14), and "that the spirit may be saved" (1 Cor. 5:5). The last clause refers to the incestuous Corinthian whom Paul told the church to put out of membership. Restoration was the goal Paul wished to see achieved through excommunication.

That the brother did repent seems clear from Paul's second letter to the Corinthians. Perhaps on the arrival of his first letter, the church took action which had its desired effect. In fact, they may have been too harsh in their treatment and too slow to welcome back the offender, for Paul writes, "Sufficient to such a man is this punishment, which was inflicted on many. So that contrariwise ye ought rather to forgive him, and comfort him, lest perhaps such a one should be swallowed up with overmuch sorrow" (2 Cor. 2:6-7).

## How to Stay Out of Court

Because of the recent rash of lawsuits brought against churches who discipline wayward members, churches are wondering how they may perform their duty of disfellowshipping members without incurring legal action and without the expense of buying malpractice insurance. Realizing that no one can be completely exempt from a charge of liability by those who wish to claim slander, libel, invasion of privacy, emotional distress, or outrageous action, the church can take steps to protect itself from frivolous lawsuits, even without compromising biblical principals. Buzzard and Brandon give several suggestions in a chapter titled "Staying Out Of Court" (*Church Discipline and the Courts*, Tyndale, 1987, pp. 235–248). Also, J. Carl Laney, associate professor at Western Conservative Baptist Seminary, speaks to the matter in an excellent article in *Christianity Today* titled, "Church Discipline without a Lawsuit" (Nov. 9, 1984, p. 76).

Here is some of their legal advice:

1. Put church members on notice concerning the practice of discipline. Spell out clearly in the church constitution the procedures and biblical foundation.

2. Incorporate into the church covenant an agreement not to seek legal action against the church or its officers in pursuance of their duties. Add a statement showing the wrongness of going to law against a brother, based on 1 Corinthians 6:1-8.

3. Require those seeking membership to familiarize themselves with the church constitution and covenant, and the steps the church will follow in handling discipline, reminding them they will be expected to abide by such procedures.

4. Show prospective members that they are entering into a covenant to care for one another's spiritual needs. Since this covenant is entered into by mutual consent, it could be terminated only by mutual consent. This should help preclude resignation as a way of avoiding discipline.

5. Make discipline the subject of preaching and adult class discussion from time to time.

6. Practice church discipline in accord with the church's governing documents and teachings. Consistency will put the courts on notice that entanglements in the life of the church constitutes interference in the free exercise of religion. Strict adherence will ward off accusations of partiality in application of discipline. Play by the rules for everyone.

7. Respect confidentiality. Except in certain instances, do not disclose matters given in confidence. However, if a counselor learns from a counselee of his intent to harm another,

the counselor is duty-bound to inform the endangered party. Also, child abuse cases should be reported. If counseling proves ineffective to halt continuing, destructive conduct, the counselor from a spiritual standpoint may need to bring the hidden into the open.

8. Limit the awareness of the church disciplinary action. It should not be reported outside one own's church. When a disciplined brother tries to join another church, only then should information of the disciplinary action be given to outsiders.

9. Keep the disclosure of facts to your own members, not outsiders. It is unwise to handle such matters during a Sunday service when visitors are likely to be present. If visitors happen to be in a business meeting when an offense is about to be discussed, dismiss them in a diplomatic manner. The command to "rebuke before all" (1 Tim. 5:20) may be limited to elders who need discipline.

10. Restrict the scope of the information disclosed. Be discreet, dealing only with current matters. Generally, fewer details need be told the congregation than a small board. Sometimes, naming a specific sin may be unnecessary. A general statement like "violating New Testament standards" may suffice in many instances.

11. Should a lawsuit be filed, by all means try to secure an out-of-court settlement. Christian lawyers are available today through the Christian Conciliation Service who will try to resolve the conflict and seek reconciliation.

12. Keep in mind that church discipline makes you and your church vulnerable. Though you may follow all these precautions, you still may be sued. But regardless of the outcome, your heart will be blameless before God, and perhaps, ultimately, in the life of the offender-plaintiff the process may still someday result in repentance, and thus banishment lead to blessing.

# 9.

## Potshots at
## Preachers and People

Tongue in cheek, Mark Twain once wrote of two cages. In the first was placed a cat, then some doves, then a dog, then a rabbit, a fox, a goose, a squirrel, and finally a monkey. In the other cage was positioned an Irish Catholic from Tipperary, a Scots Presbyterian from Aberdeen, a Turk, a Greek Christian, an Armenian, a Methodist, a Buddhist, a Brahman, and then a Salvation Army colonel. Two days later the animals were living in peace. But the second cage was a "chaos of gory odds and ends of turbans and fezzes and plaids and bones and flesh—not a specimen alive." According to Mark Twain, these reasoning animals had fought over a theological detail, then had carried the matter to a higher court.

Though believers are to contend for the faith, they are not to be contentious. Too often feuding and fighting lead to great damage. The writer of Hebrews commanded, "Follow peace with all men, and holiness . . . lest any root of bitterness springing up trouble you, and thereby many be defiled" (12:15).

### Leaders against Leaders
*Newsweek* for June 8, 1987 began a major article two months after the PTL scandal broke:

119

Sleazy and sordid and endlessly fascinating, evangelism's Holy War degenerated into a televised mudslinging contest last week. The battle raged nearly around the clock—from "Good Morning America" to the evening news to the highlights at 11 and the low blows on "Nightline," where the religion-sex-money scandal made the ratings soar. The Rev. Jerry Falwell . . . sneered at the excuses offered by Jim Bakker, the defrocked and disgraced charismatic preacher. . . . Bakker accused Falwell of lying and "stealing" his ministry, the lucrative PTL television empire and the Heritage USA Christian resort (p. 58).

Jamie Buckingham, writing in *Charisma* magazine, commented on a meeting in March 1987 of over 600 Christian leaders in Kansas City to search for ethical excellence in fundraising:

The conference closed with [prayer] for Oral Roberts, [the one praying] asking God to "bring him into repentance if he is wrong." Not long afterward, Oral was in his prayer tower, calling on Jimmy Swaggart to repent. Swaggart, down in Baton Rouge, was demanding that Jim Bakker and Richard Dortch repent. Maybe, with all these calls for repentance, some leader will look into his own heart and pick up the cry of the publican in the temple: "God, be merciful to ME, the sinner" (June 1987, p. 22).

In March 1987 Marvin Gorman filed a $90 million lawsuit against Jimmy Swaggart, the Assemblies of God denomination, and others, claiming that Swaggart urged Bakker to remove from the PTL network all TV program time of Marvin Gorman Ministries. A Swaggart spokesman replied, "Every allegation in his suit, whether it be against us, the Assemblies, or anyone else, is an absolute baldface lie" (*Charisma*, June 1987, p. 62).

An AP release in June 1987, reporting a drop in contributions in the aftermath of the Bakker episode, also "blamed the Rev. Oral Roberts for pleadings that he might die this spring if he did not meet a fund-raising target."

## Reformers Fought in a Similar Fashion

Great and godly as were the church reformers of the sixteenth century, they were guilty of heaping invective on leaders who held opposing views. Philip Schaff, a careful historian, described Martin Luther's debating disposition in these words: "His writings smell of powder; his words are battles; he overwhelms his opponents with a roaring cannonade of argument, eloquence, passion, and abuse."

Five years after praising Erasmus, Luther called him "the vainest creature in the world, an enraged viper, a refined Epicurean, a scoffer, and a disguised atheist" (Arthur H. Matthews, "Where the Reformers Stumbled" in *Christianity Today*, Oct. 24, 1975, p. 7).

Luther insulted Zwingli by deliberately and repeatedly misspelling his name. He piled such vulgarity on him that Schaff said he could not translate its meaning into decent English. That such verbal abuse was commonplace in that day still did not make it innocent and harmless.

Preserved in an old German monastery are two pairs of deer horns interlocked, said to have been found in that position many years ago. The deer had been fighting when their horns jammed together and could not be separated. They died with locked horns. Said one historian, "I would like to take those horns into every house and school in the country." And we would add, "And into every church."

How tragic that members of the same church body could be linked for mutual destruction. Does any part of the human body fight against any other member? Does hand pluck out eye, or leg kick ankle? Fighting among believers in any age carries a high price tag. Just as in war both victor and vanquished pay a tremendous cost, so battle among brethren incurs mutual spiritual injury. Offensive language and malicious action destroy friendships, tear down reputations, and consume churches. It seems incredible to us today that the

Reformers actually in some instances drowned Anabaptists because the Anabaptists insisted so strongly that baptism was only for believers. Reformers took so-called heretics, totaling thousands, placed them in weighted bags, and tossed them to watery graves.

## Modern Instances

In addition to the widely publicized Bakker controversy and its aftershocks, potshots are constantly fired today by leaders of one faction, criticizing leaders of other viewpoints for not holding to the party line. Certain journals major in denouncing, or smearing by association, the leaders of their own or other denominations for the speakers the leaders invite to their churches or conventions, for the platforms to which they lend their presence, and for the crusades to which they give their support.

A respected Sunday School take-home paper for boys and girls some years ago innocently recounted in a cartoon strip how a Chinese landowner turned the other cheek when the town leader took over certain land; the editors sincerely intended to illustrate application of Jesus' admonition in Matthew 5:39. A certain state publication of an ultraconservative denomination published a scathing attack on the evangelical publishing house, accusing it of peddling Communist propaganda—without any contact whatsoever with the editors or executives of the publisher to determine the facts.

A preacher who did not feel constrained to withdraw from a certain denomination was not only severely roasted in the press by pastors disagreeing with him, but many a Sunday morning, just a few minutes before entering the pulpit, he would be handed a telegram from a pastor in another city blasting him for his disloyalty to Scripture. Needless to say, such messages wreaked havoc with the spirit of worship with which the preacher had planned to enter the pulpit.

In another case, a proponent of separation from modernistic denominations printed his so-called all-star teams of liberal leaders. On the first team he placed the names of leaders who definitely espoused denial of cardinal Christian truths. However, he made his second modernist team consist of irreproachable evangelical leaders who believed the main fundamentals, but whose unpardonable sin was that they had not broken their denominational ties.

When evangelist Jack Van Impe accepted an invitation to speak at Moody Bible Institute's Founders Week Conference in 1972, he was warned by telegram from the committee in charge of his scheduled Chicago crusade that, if he participated in the Moody conference, they would cancel the crusade. Van Impe decided not to speak at Moody's Founders Conference. Yet, the same men who threatened to cancel the crusade drove Van Impe to WMBI each morning to promote the crusade services over the Bible school's radio station. Airtime was offered free of charge through the kindness of WMBI leaders.

## Paul's Experience

The history of leaders taking potshots at other leaders goes all the way back to Paul's time. False leaders at Corinth had accused Paul of cowardly weakness and lack of effectiveness, of not possessing a full knowledge of Christ and of the true Gospel, and of accepting no salary because he knew he was an imposter. In 2 Corinthians 10-13 Paul answered these charges in order. In chapter 10 he claimed divine power be measured by actual achievement and not by empty bragging, power that he would exercise, if necessary, upon his arrival in Corinth.

In 11:1-6 he defended the pure Gospel which he most certainly preached. Then from 11:7 through chapter 13 he gave his reasons for refusing pay for his missionary labors. He ended his defense with a warning to the false teachers. Yes, Paul knew what it was to be the object of potshots.

## Parishioners Against Pastors

Seemingly, congregations are dismissing pastors in unprecedented numbers today. In the book *Forced Termination*, dealing with the problems of ministers fired or forced to resign, the author says, "It is happening among Baptists, Methodists, Presbyterians, Episcopalians, Church of the Brethren, Christian churches, and every denomination in the United States—and even the world. Some have called it an 'epidemic' " (Brooks R. Faulkner, Broadman, 1986, p. 8).

One stunned minister told me on the phone that he had been summarily dismissed without advance warning for giving an altar call, having a missionary speak in the morning service, and using too many sermon illustrations.

One minister realized some people in his church definitely wanted him to leave when they poisoned his daughter's horse.

Why are ministers dismissed at seemingly higher frequency? Many factors are involved. They receive a minimum of feedback, thus often oblivious to the true state of affairs. An oversupply of ministers makes a church independent in its attitude. Some churches receive over a hundred resumes when their pulpits are vacant. The restlessness of our day gives rise to church crises. The frenzied pace and pressures of living often spill over into church activities. Congregations sometimes have too high expectations of their pastor. How does a pastor of a small church compare with the talented TV celebrity who comes across so smoothly in the living rooms of that pastor's parishioners?

But perhaps as significant as any of the above factors is the lower level of respect given pastors today. Such behavior neglects the biblical imperative, "Respect those who work hard among you, who are over you in the Lord and who admonish you. Hold them in the highest regard in love because of their work" (1 Thes. 5:12-13, NIV). Then as if to show that such honor will help avoid conflict, Paul adds, "Live in peace with each other." Three times in the last chapter of Hebrews, the writer enjoins respect, even obedience, of leaders (13:7, 17). When my mother observed pastors mistreated, she would quote David's words, who, when he was unjustly hounded by King Saul and had opportunity to kill him, replied to his advisors: "Who can stretch forth his hand against the Lord's anointed, and be guiltless? (1 Sam. 26:9)

## Typical Parishioner Potshots

A farmer asked a restaurant owner if he could use a million frog legs. Desirous of putting frog legs on the menu more frequently, the owner asked where the farmer could get so many. He replied, "My pond is overflowing with them. Their croaking is driving me up the wall." The restauranteur ordered several hundred frogs. A week later the farmer returned to the restaurant with a sheepish look on his face. "I was wrong about a million frog legs." Holding two scrawny frogs, he admitted, "These two little frogs were making all the racket. I never knew two little frogs could sound like a million!"

Many a congregation has had a couple of croakers who complained enough for a hundred people, never helping but always hindering. Then dozens of others are ready to snipe, either directly at the pastor or indirectly behind his back. Do these potshots sound familiar?

— "I'm not being fed."
— "Your sermons don't have depth. They're not meeting my needs."
— "I tried to call you on your day off, Pastor. You know, my husband rarely takes a day off."
— "I've come to share a personal concern."
— "I want you to know the real situation."
— "You're not reaching people as effectively as you did a year ago."
— "Aren't you trying to build an empire?"
— "Setting goals is too much like the world."
— "Why reach out for more people when we're not doing a good job with those we have."
— "Why are you speaking at that Bible conference? Don't you know we pay you to be pastor here?"
— "You tell too many stories."
— "You don't use enough illustrations."
— "You counsel too much."
— "We need more solid Bible teaching."
— "We need more evangelistic messages."

— "We need more sermons on money." (This from a reluctant tither peeved that other members are not assuming their share of the financial load.)

— "They sure don't make pastors like they used to."

— "I don't like the direction the church is taking."

— "You need to preach more forcefully."

— "The church seems to have lost its first love."

— "You need to be more of a leader."

— "Your sermons aren't challenging."

— "You need to take a stronger stand against the world."

— "You preach from a Bible version I dislike."

— "Our shepherding program is worthless."

— "I wonder if our pastor prays enough."

— "Why doesn't our church do something for the poor?"

— "We need to pray for our pastor. He needs help, you know. He's got big problems."

— "The pastor never visits."

## Handling Potshots

A pastor wondered why one of his staunch supporters began to turn cool. Though he visited this supporting member's father in the nursing home regularly, illness and fading memory caused the father to remark to his son, "Why doesn't the pastor ever visit me?" When this complaint was voiced several times, the son began to wonder about the pastor's faithfulness in calling. After the pastor learned of the situation, he started the practice of sending a brief note to the son after every visit. Then he extended the practice by sending a brief note to the son or daughter of every older parishioner visited in the hospital or nursing home or other institution. Defending the expenditure of time and money on this project, he retorted, "It's cheaper than malpractice insurance."

One pastor published quarterly in the church bulletin the number of visits made in homes, hospitals, and other institutions the previous three months, thus showing that he was indeed a "visiting" pastor.

The charge, "Pastor, I'm not getting the depth from your

sermons that I need," has reached the level of a catchphrase which can easily be turned into a weapon. Its vagueness makes defense frustrating. In *Leadership* magazine, Pastor Joel C. Hunter suggests three possible meanings. First, the critic may mean he wishes more detail rather than depth, such as the meaning of the original language and social and historical background. Or the critic may mean he wants a sermon to have a clear call for action, application, and accountability. Or the critic may feel a sermon is incomplete unless it makes the hearer squirm under the conviction of the Holy Spirit. Recapping, depth may mean detail, application, or conviction (*Spring Quarter* 1987, pp. 48–50). Possibly, the preacher needs to brush up in one or more of these areas.

In any event, a wise pastor will not fire potshots back at his critic, especially from the pulpit, but will carefully evaluate the barb. Whatever is unjustifiable, he will quietly forget. Whatever is legitimate, he will take to heart and try to correct. Maybe the Lord is trying to say something to the pastor. I well remember, some years ago, a letter handed me by a supportive woman in our church just as I was to walk out to the platform for the morning service. Opening it up for a quick glance in case there was something I should have known before the service, I noted it contained criticisms of recent sermons. The sermons were shallow, she scolded, and I used too many illustrations. Without mentioning the letter to anyone, I heeded its contents and paid attention to the quality of my sermons from then on. A year later I quietly asked the same woman how my sermons were coming across. "Oh," she replied, "I'd almost forgotten about that letter. I haven't heard any criticism for a long time."

Criticism may be painfully unfair. A study of pastoral dropout reveals that a high percentage of preachers who leave the ministry within five years of ordination do so because their idealism has been worn thin by frustrating encounters with church members who are stubborn, selfish, and immature. Instead of discussing the matter with the pastor, parishioners either attack him openly or dissect him covertly.

## Parishioners Versus Parishioners

Much church conflict arises when believers who lack love become petty, personal, and pugnacious with other believers. Instead of facing the issue, they assault each other with their tongues. Someone has said that the quality of conversation, in descending rank, is about ideas, then things, then people. It has been suggested that Adam and Eve had a hard time making conversation when they had no one to talk about.

James says it simply, "Speak not evil one of another, brethren" (4:11). And, "Grudge not one against another, brethren" (5:9). Both involve the wrong of judging which may take many forms: knocking, mudslinging, gossip, jumping to conclusions, backbiting, slandering, caustic criticism, and detraction. By judging we not only usurp the prerogative of God, who alone knows all the facts, but we may do irreparable harm to fellow believers. A teenager who had recently accepted Christ at a church meeting was introduced to another Christian fellow who proceeded to voice a careless criticism of the preacher. Sadly, the new convert showed no subsequent interest in the church.

Roast beef makes a good Sunday dinner, but not roast preacher. Many children hearing their parents take potshots at the pastor at Sunday meals have later refused to listen to him either in public preaching or private counsel. Neither should we serve roast Sunday School teacher, roast organist, or roast soloist. We cannot build up the Lord's work while tearing down His workers. Though a little thing, the untamed tongue has crushed hearts, divided families, and split churches.

A good many of our name-calling, sinister insinuations and devilish detractions spring from envy. When someone makes a substantial gift to the church, the envious speculates: "He's trying to escape the income tax." After a Christian buys new furniture, a neighbor comments, "I don't know how they do it unless they don't tithe. We'd have a lot more money to spend if we didn't tithe."

## Consuming Each Other

A man bitten by a dog became violently ill, so goes a story. The doctor explained, "You've been bitten by a rabid dog, and you are dying of hydrophobia. There's nothing I can do for you." The stricken man asked for a pencil and paper, then spent several minutes thinking and writing. About to leave, the doctor said, "You certainly are making a lengthy will." Retorted the patient, "I'm not making my will; I'm making a list of people I'm going to bite."

A recent *National Geographic* magazine carried the photograph of the fossil remains of two saber-toothed cats who died locked in mortal combat. One had bitten so deeply into the other cat's leg that it could not remove its teeth. Its powerful thrust trapped both animals in a common fate. How reminiscent of Paul's warning to the Galatians, "But if ye bite and devour one another, take heed that ye be not consumed one of another" (5:15).

Two little sisters had a nasty spat, and their mother told them this story. Once upon a time there were two cats: one black with a white tip on his black tail and the other white with the tip of his tail black. Said the mother, "These cats were always fighting. When the white cat lay sleeping cozily before the fire, and the black cat entered the room, up would leap the white cat with back arched and tail fluffed out, hissing and spitting and calling the black cat all kinds of names. He acted exactly like two little girls I know."

Joyce and Jean looked at each other, but Mother went on as if she hadn't noticed. "One day some of the boys saw the cats fighting in the backyard. They tied the two cats together by the ends of their tails, hung them over the clothesline, and left them. By morning they'll have their fill of fighting, thought the boys. But when the boys came back in the morning, there was nothing left but the tips of two tails, one black and the other white. They had eaten each other up!"

"O mother," giggled Joyce. "They couldn't have done that! How could they keep eating without any mouths?"

"No," agreed mother, "they couldn't, of course. That's just

a story. But little girls sometimes say biting things to each other, until they've left nothing good of each other at all. For instance, each of you had said tonight that the other was selfish; and worse than that, that the other was lying. So you've 'eaten up' each other's unselfishness and truthfulness. This afternoon I heard you say, 'You mean thing!' So your kindness is eaten up too. I'm afraid that someday I'll find no goodness left in my girls. It will all be eaten up—just badness left."

Vindictive strife shakes the sanctuary. Chris Lyons, in a sermon a few years ago at the Wheaton (Ill.) Bible Church, said, "I know of churches which had a great testimony and where many were saved, but conflict came in. The church split. And never again through the years has that been a great church or had many people saved. These churches go on for a generation with all the scars and hurts; they seem never to get over it."

Division over a substantial doctrine may sometimes be necessary, even beneficial, but God never promised to bless a church divided through interpersonal strife. Petty, prolonged internal wrangling has diminished or extinguished the light of many a once-radiant congregation.

A twenty-five-year-old upstate New York church, which through a series of quarrels devoured its membership till only seven were left, was about to close its doors. A denominational director received a phone call from the lone surviving deacon to see if his denomination would take the church over. The director, finally decided "Ichabod" had been written over this building because the local residents had generally come to regard the church as a place of which it could be said, "Behold how they fight with one another." How essential for believers to strive to keep the unity of the faith.

## Reaction to Potshots
Pastors would do well to react as follows to faultfinding:
— Don't hurl back potshots in retaliation. Don't answer venom with venom.

— Permit others to state their disagreements.
— Listen well. Try to understand a critic's position, appreciating his strongest points.
— Emphasize agreements.
— Give credit for sincerity.
— Don't categorize an adversary.
— Remember you might possibly be mistaken.
— Don't hold a grudge or become bitter.
— Pray for those from whom you differ.
— Be always gentle, though firm. As we show people the mind of Christ, we build unity.

## All-Conquering Love

In the verse before the warning against consuming one another, Paul reminds, "Thou shalt love thy neighbor as thyself" (Gal. 5:14). Malice consumes but love conserves, turning incipient friction into cementing fellowship. And, when the outside world sees compassion among Christians, they become convinced of the genuineness of Christianity. As Jesus said, "By this shall all men know that ye are My disciples, if ye have love one to another" (John 13:35). Happily, some churches have proved the truth and power of this reality.

Early one Monday morning some years ago Pastor Virgil Savage of the First Baptist Church of Redmond, Oregon sensed trouble when he answered his phone. His Sunday School superintendent, voice irritated and insistent, said, "There's something I want to talk to you about in your study this morning."

When his burly superintendent showed up a few minutes later, the pastor could tell all was not well. The superintendent had some personal matters between them that needed airing. Settling their differences in a Christian manner, they prayed together. Then Pastor Savage suggested they meet for prayer the next morning.

They began to meet regularly. In time, men joined them. Thus began a daily 6:30 A.M. prayer meeting which was to result in the winning of many men to Christ. One convert was the town butcher, Dan Lawler, a tough, cigar-chewing, whiskey-drinking merchant who was proud of his combination meat market and cold-storage locker business. Soon cigars and whiskey disappeared from Lawler's life, while a growing interest in the Bible led him to sell his flourishing business and move to Portland to attend a Bible institute and seminary.

A burden for starting a new church in an unchurched area led Lawler to found the Gateway Baptist Church. Then he felt the burden for starting another church. Through his leadership during the next several years, seventeen building projects were completed with the aid of involved laymen. Lawler's talents were invested statewide as he served for years as director of church extension for the Conservative Baptist Association of Oregon. The urge to plant another new church led him back to pioneer what has become another fast-growing church.

Interestingly, the man who took over the first church he started, Gateway Baptist, was none other than the Sunday School superintendent, one of the original pair who started the prayer meeting.

It all came about as a result of two men meeting to solve their differences, and then joining in fellowship and prayer.

The psalmist said, "Behold, how good and how pleasant it is for brethren to dwell together in unity! (133:1)

Perhaps the way to win those inevitable church fights is to give in—to the Holy Spirit, and watch Him restore unity and power to the church.

# 10.
# The Strong Versus the Weak

The late Dr. Percy Crawford, youth evangelist and founder of The King's College, was holding services throughout Korea, accompanied by his quartet. To reach a church service in Pusan scheduled for next morning, they traveled by train over Saturday night and into the early hours of Sunday. When they arrived, they were told the service had been cancelled. At first, church officials wouldn't give any reason, but finally told him it was because they had traveled on a train on Sunday.

As I sat on the platform of an auditorium one September morning, waiting to give a message at a Christian college faculty retreat, I noticed several faculty members walk in, sporting full-grown beards. The dean leaned over and whispered, "Tomorrow, when the students arrive for orientation, I have to tell them that they are not permitted to wear beards. The rule does not apply to faculty and staff." At that moment I remembered seeing pictures of D.L. Moody, founder of Moody Bible Institute, and of A.B. Simpson, founder of Nyack College, and of other Christian stalwarts of nearly a century ago, each wearing a luxurious beard. In fact, I had read that in most Western communities in the roaring '90s smooth-faced men were run out of town.

More than one church dispute has flared over whether

133

certain cultural practices should be allowed or banned. The early church at Rome had a couple of such problems, and though they seem trivial or ridiculous to us today, they involved important principles and were edging the church toward a serious rift.

## The Issues

Most of the Roman populace, except for the Jews and the Christians, worshiped idols. At banquets and other celebrations, meat was often served that had been dedicated to idols in the temples before being taken to the markets for public sale. Converted Jews, who continued to adhere to the Mosaic code regulating food they could eat, and who deplored idols, insisted that Christians could have nothing to do with such meat, even though it often was of highest quality.

These folks were not like the Judaizers who made salvation dependent on something added to faith, or else Paul would have rebuked them severely. But their "weak" consciences caused them to continue to observe Jewish dietary laws.

Most Gentile believers at Rome were rejoicing in their Christ-given liberation. They rejected idol worship, but they did not see anything immoral in eating meat previously dedicated in the temples since they knew an idol was nothing but a piece of carved wood or stone. So they ate meat whenever they pleased. Their consciences were clear; to them meat-eating was a matter of moral indifference.

Paul spoke of these two groups: "For one believeth that he may eat all things: another, who is weak, eateth herbs" (Rom. 14:2). The same two groups differed over another issue: Sabbath observance. Those who observed the Jewish dietary laws and abstained from meat also followed the Jewish law of the Sabbath. Those who didn't come from Jewish background weren't likely to keep the Sabbath. Paul wrote, "One man esteemeth one day above another; another esteemeth every day alike" (14:5).

With these two groups holding opposite viewpoints, and each deeming itself more spiritual than the other, the stage was set for trouble. The meat-eater despised the abstainer. And equally, the abstainer passed judgment on the eater. Paul pinpointed this mutual censure and uncharitable judgment that had likely already strained the fellowship (14:1-3). Recognizing the rightness in each position, Paul rebuked both for their critical disparagement of the other.

Wide disagreements exist today in our churches over certain practices. Scruples vary in different parts of our country and world. (A scruple has been explained as an opinion without concrete biblical support, like the judgment that men should wear neckties to church, or that ladies should not wear pantsuits to Sunday services.)

Some Christians think they should never patronize a commercial theater. Others believe that they can, but that they should be selective with their movies just as they are with their literature. When Corrie ten Boom's *The Hiding Place* was shown in the regular theaters, one Christian college in the East forbade its students even to attend, much less help out as counselors or ushers. But most believers found no problem with attending or staffing the movie.

A Christian couple having moved from the South was surprised when an evangelical church announced a swimming party for the couples' club for the next Saturday. As they stood outside the church after the service, explaining to a member why they disapproved of mixed bathing, the husband offended his Northern brother by lighting up a cigarette.

A Christian from western Canada thought it worldly for a Christian acquaintance to wear her wedding ring, while a woman from Europe thought it almost immoral for a wife not to wear a ring that signaled her status, lest she invite illicit male advances.

A man from Denmark was pained even to watch British Bible school students play football, while the British students shrank from the Dane's pipe smoking.

A German believer said to a U.S. visitor, "I grieve for you Americans. When I think of all the harm you are doing to yourselves by smoking, I could cry in my beer."

## When the Saints Come Storming In

Some groups forbid lipstick, but permit the use of powder. A woman told a gathering that it was wrong to wear earrings, but as she spoke, three rows of pearls encircled her neck and bracelets dangled from both wrists.

One pastor refused to support an evangelistic crusade unless team members refrained from wearing wire-rimmed glasses, which he felt were a sign of "hippyism."

Many a congregation, as William Barclay puts it, has been "torn in two because those who hold broader and more liberal views are angrily contemptuous of those whom they regard as stick-in-the-mud, die-hard conservatives and puritans; and because those who are stricter in their outlook are critical, censorious, and condemning of those who wish the right to do things which they think are wrong" (*The Letter to the Romans*, Westminster Press, p. 199).

Conflict in the church at Rome had intensified to the point, conjectures one scholar, where "probably the church refused membership to those who held eccentric views," so Paul was seeking to avoid further schism (Davidson, Stibbs and Kevan, *The New Bible Commentary*, Eerdmans, 1953, p. 962).

Contention from this disagreement still persisted a few years later when Paul arrived in Rome as a prisoner of the emperor. From his own hired house, Paul wrote in the Philippian letter that some Roman Christians were proclaiming Christ out of envy, strife, and contention (1:15-16). The faction that insisted on observing Old Testament ceremonial laws—in direct contradiction to Paul's teaching—took advantage of his confinement to promote their viewpoint and thus distress Paul.

Unbelievable as it seems, fairly substantial evidence suggests that strife between these two groups was responsible for the martyrdom of many Roman Christians. Near the end of the first century, a Christian leader in Rome, Clement, wrote a letter to the church in Corinth. His main thrust was to reprimand a spirit of envy and animosity in the Corinthian church. To show the dire consequences of such strife, Clement indicated that about the time of Paul's incarceration a vast number of believers had been martyred because of jealousy ("Epistle of Clement to the Corinthians," in *Apostolic Fathers,* Baker, 1956, p. 15).

Theologian Oscar Cullman, in his book *Peter,* concludes that these martyrs (and he includes Paul and Peter) were victims of jealous strife from persons who counted themselves members of the Christian church at Rome. Rivalry between factions at the capital became so bitter that some brethren handed in names of their Christian opponents as traitors to the empire. After sifting the evidence, Cullman sadly concludes that envy among Christians helped feed saints to the lions in the coliseum and lit fires under Christian brethren in Nero's gardens. What terrible conflagrations can rise from spiteful sparks! (Westminster Press, pp. 101-109)

Cullman also suggests that the abrupt ending of the book of Acts with Paul a prisoner at Rome may be explained by the painful circumstances that contributed to these many martyrdoms. Perhaps Luke, who authored Acts, wished to pull a curtain over this grievous strife among God's people. Clement, on the other hand, wanted to warn the Corinthian church a generation later what dangers threatened any church that allowed similar dissension to go unchecked.

## To Do or Not to Do

Paul classified the two factions at Rome as "the strong" and "the weak," or the convinced and the doubters. The strong were those who ate meat and disregarded the Sabbath, convinced such practices were proper. The weak, doubtful about such matters, abstained from meat and observed the day. Today, we often erroneously reverse Paul's characterization, considering the abstainers the strong and the eaters the weak. However, the wrong was plainly not in the controversial action, but in the injured consciences and the animosity that smothered love in the fellowship. Because each group was vulnerable to specific failings, Paul gave explicit instruction to both.

- *To the strong: Do not despise the weak.* In many life

137

situations the strong are tempted to disdain the weak. The boy who can run faster, throw faster, and lift more tends to scorn the one who cannot do as well. Spiritually strong people tend to look down on the weak, regarding them as ignorant, fanatic, or scrupulous. What the weak need is loving acceptance. "Accept the one who is weak in the faith," Paul directed (Rom. 14:1, NASB).

Weak believers should be accepted readily into church membership. The church is not a club for perfect people, but a school for the spiritually illiterate to learn and a hospital for the spiritually ill to be made well. New and weak Christians should be welcomed for training in reliance on the Lord, not for indoctrination in matters of moral indifference.

● *To the weak: Do not judge the strong.* The command not to judge another in matters of moral indifference is strongly emphasized (Rom. 14:3-4, 10-13). Why judge a person whom God has accepted? How contrary to common sense to judge another man's servant—that's his master's job. So, leave the judging of fellow servants to God, which is His responsibility, not ours, especially since both eater and abstainer act as unto the Lord.

Too often we play God by trying to make others conform to our standards. A woman spent ten minutes telling a friend she shouldn't wear makeup, wedding rings, or lipstick. About to leave, she added, "By the way, I see your hair is getting gray on the side. Why don't you touch it up with some dye? I'll tell you what brand I use."

Each person, strong or weak, confident or uncertain, must decide for himself and become fully persuaded in his own mind under the leadership of Christ. Since personalities, needs, and opportunities differ, our conclusions will vary on morally debatable practices. We must not dogmatically force our scruples on others so that believers become cookie-cutter, assembly-line, mass-produced reproductions of every other Christian. Dr. J. Gresham Machen counseled Christians to keep their consciences free from "the tyranny of experts." Not conformity to the crowd, but conviction of heart, informed by the principles of God's Word, should decide these questionable matters.

Does a custom or practice appear evil to you? Avoid it and let other Christians answer to God, not to you.

● *To the strong: Respect the weak brother's conscience.* But the confident-strong are not off Paul's hook yet. They can be wrong in doing a right action. Paul warns the strong against flaunting their liberty. Such freedom in the presence of the weak may induce an uncertain-weak brother to do something his conscience says is wrong. Violation of one's conscience is moral failure and an obstacle in the path of spiritual progress. For the strong to so influence a weak brother is to destroy the work of God (Rom. 14:20). Instead, Paul advises, "Follow after the things which make for peace, and things wherewith one may edify another" (v. 19).

At least three social situations involving the eating of meat had to be faced by New Testament believers at Rome and elsewhere: (1) in a temple in sight of an idol; (2) at home when the meat had been purchased in the marketplace without knowledge of whether or not it had been offered to an idol; and (3) at a friend's house when it was pointed out that the meat had been previously sacrificed in a temple. Paul handled these problems in writing the Corinthians. The same advice would pertain at Rome.

The first instance is forbidden, for eating meat in the shadow of an idol goes too far (1 Cor. 10:20-21).

The second circumstance should cause no anxiety. Whether or not meat sold in the marketplace had been sacrificed to an idol is unimportant to a believer. Buy what is sold in the market and ask no questions (1 Cor. 10:25-26).

The third case is more complex—the question of eating meat at a friend's house. If no one makes an issue of it, all should eat (1 Cor. 10:27). But if a scrupulous believer points out to you that the meat has been offered before an idol, thus confronting your influence on him, Paul advises abstinence (1 Cor. 10:28-29).

True knowledge enables a believer to eat meat previously offered to an idol without having his conscience troubled. But

Paul warns that knowledge must be tempered by love. Knowledge puffs up, but love builds up. In the midst of a believing community, the viewpoint of other believers must be taken into consideration. Paul's words to the Roman Christians can fit many similar situations today: "Let us not judge one another any more, but rather determine this—not to put an obstacle or a stumbling block in a brother's way. . . . For if because of food your brother is hurt, you are not longer walking according to love. Do not destroy with your food him for whom Christ died. . . . It is good not to eat meat or to drink wine, or to do anything by which your brother stumbles" (14:13, 15, 21, NASB). Are you truly strong? Then bear with the burdens of the weak.

● *To the weak: Grow up.* An eye-catching drawing in a magazine depicted a muscular man holding a picture of himself before he developed his physique. The picture pointed up the title of an article, "Don't Be a 95-Pound Christian Weakling!" The article began by reminding us how often we have heard sermons on the responsibility of treating a weaker brother with love lest we lead him to fall. Though such advice is scriptural and needed, author William Coleman says, "The time has come to address the weaker brother, 'Why don't you grow up and stop being so easily offended?' " (*Eternity*, March 1975, p. 15) The strong brother need not become a prisoner of a weak brother's conscience, but should expect the weakling to become mature.

Good point. If "the weaker brother" is a person who expects others to live by his scruples and becomes uptight when others do not comply, his faith is feeble. The weak brother who has to be handled with kid gloves when others do things that don't suit him should ask the Lord for help to develop into a healthy, robust believer, and thus join the ranks of the stronger brethren.

## Incentives to Accepting Each Other
Sixteenth-century theologian Melanchthon put it well: "In essentials, unity; in nonessentials, liberty; in all things,

charity." Here are some of Paul's reasons for not excluding, but welcoming one another.

• *Because both factions belong to the Lord.* The one who observes a particular day regards it unto the Lord. The one who fails to observe a day is likewise seeking to honor the same Lord. Both meat-eater and abstainer give thanks to the same God (Rom. 14:6). Thus, both have a common Lord, seek a common goal, escape a common danger through a common salvation, and find themselves in a common ark where differences fade into relative unimportance.

• *Because matters of moral indifference do not constitute Christianity.* A twenty-year-old girl confessed, "When I was first converted, I honestly thought that all Christian girls should wear their dresses to their ankles, long hair down their backs, and always carry a Bible. I was even indignant when I saw Christians reading secular books. The Lord soon began to remind me that all Christendom wasn't required to live up to my pious standards! I had to surrender my self-righteous attitude and realize that God was more concerned with a person's heart attitude. Nothing is wrong with dresses down to the ankle or carrying a Bible everywhere, but every Christian girl doesn't have to do it."

Paul wrote, "For the kingdom of God is not meat and drink, but righteousness, and peace, and joy in the Holy Ghost" (Rom. 14:17). He could have added to the list of what Christianity is not: rings, or cosmetics, or TV, or guitars, or a host of other practices where Scripture does not take a stand, and in which we must be flexible. Neither our standing before God nor inner peace nor joyous spirit is dependent on matters of moral indifference. We must not confuse lifestyle with humility, compassion, purity and peaceableness.

• *Because Christ has received us.* A missionary in the days of the Belgian Congo condemned a fad spreading through his congregation which involved mixing crushed mothballs with palm oil and using the preparation as a kind of cologne or perfume. To stop the fad, the church appointed men to sniff out those wearing the mothball preparation and refuse them entrance to service. Though most American church leaders would never practice sniffing their members at the door of the church, yet do we not often in our minds reject people on the basis of some practice? Paul wrote, "Wherefore receive ye one another, as Christ also received us" (Rom. 15:7). Just as Christ accepted us when we were unlovely, without strength, and un-Christlike, so we should willingly welcome those who are "weak brethren" and indulging in a lifestyle we don't exactly approve.

• *Because the body will be warmed in love.* An elderly lady in Massachusetts could not bear to see stray cats out in the cold winter night. One January evening she sheltered six stray cats plus her own dog and cat. After retiring she was suddenly stricken with an illness and could not get out of bed. The house grew cold as her stove fire died out. Windows rattled as the wind howled through the night. The temperature dropped to zero. It looked hopeless for this elderly lady.

When the neighbors missed her the next day, they found her lying in her bed, warm as toast. On each side of her head purred a stray cat. Another was draped like a fur piece around her neck. Two were snuggled under her armpits, and two more against her sides. Her dog lay across her stomach. The strays she had befriended had saved her life.

The church should also harbor the straying, the misfits, the sick. These outsiders, welcomed and nourished, could protect the church from a slow freeze into professionalism and formalism.

But to get the benefit of their warmth, the church must admit the weak.

# 11.

# *Ladies, Get Your Act Together*

A story is told of two unmarried sisters who had so bitter a ruckus they stopped speaking to each other. Unable or unwilling to separate, the pair lived in a large single room with two beds. A chalk line divided the sleeping area into two halves, separating doorway and fireplace, so that each could come and go and get her own meals without trespassing on her sister's domain. In the black of night each could hear the breathing of the foe. For years they coexisted in spiteful silence. Neither was willing to take the first step to reconciliation. How sad for those four walls to look down on such an unsisterly spectacle.

Two women at the church of Philippi had a rift, probably of a mild nature; but to prevent it from becoming a major rupture, Paul directed a remark to these women in his epistle to that church.

Women played an important role in the early church. Some of them gave financial support to Jesus' ministry (Luke 8:1-3). Grieving women were last at the cross and first at the tomb. In the last chapter of Romans, Paul lists twenty-seven names of co-workers, one-third of which are women's. On some mission fields today women outnumber men. Because some missionary work has been financed by the legacies of rich men, someone quipped that the missionary enterprise has been carried on by living women and dead men.

The female element loomed large in the Philippian church. Paul's first congregation was composed of women meeting by the riverside. His first convert was Lydia, a woman merchant (Acts 16:13-14). Then a demon-possessed girl was healed (v. 18). Among early members were the two women who had a falling-out, Euodias and Syntyche. Diligent co-workers of Paul's from near the beginning, they made a significant contribution in those formative years of this outstanding church.

We should not be surprised that this flourishing congregation had a spat between two of its members. Earlier chapters have shown that practically every New Testament church of which we have substantial record had controversy of one sort or another. For example, the church at Jerusalem was the scene of the church's first recorded friction due to the alleged inequality of daily handouts, and also the locale of the First Church Council. The church at Antioch suffered three serious disputes in a few short years: Paul versus Peter, Paul versus Barnabas, and the Judaizers versus the advocates of liberty. At Rome two groups had difficulty accepting each other. The Galatians were warned not to devour one another. The Ephesians were urged to keep the unity of the Spirit in the bond of peace (Eph. 4:3). The advice to the Colossians to be forbearing and forgiving if any had a quarrel against another seems to indicate the existence of discord (Col. 3:13). At Thessalonica, saints idle likely because they thought Christ's return was so near intruded into their neighbors' private business (2 Thes. 3:11). And here at Philippi two women were at cross-purposes. Apparently, conflict is unavoidable in the best of churches. Of greater importance is the proper resolution of inevitable controversy.

## Minor Tiff or Major Trauma

Somehow Satan got his claws hooked in, not so much that discord separated two warmhearted women, but that it went unmended too long. In a thriving church like Philippi, slight bickerings would rumble like thunder. Paul's appeal indicates that the difference was not simply a private matter but one that threatened the unity of the congregation.

Incidentally, this is the sole New Testament case of dissension with women as the principals. Even the first friction that involved widows brought confrontation between male Hebrews and male Hellenists.

On what did these women differ? We are not told. Conflicts can be classified under two main categories: substantive and interpersonal. Conflict occurs when two ideas or actions try to occupy the same operating space at the same time. For example, if a member asserts that the best way to evangelize is by house-to-house visitation, and another insists that joining protest marches is the proper method, conflict will result. This is substantive conflict.

Interpersonal conflict stems from incompatibility between people rather than from facts and values. Examples would be dislike of others because of racial or social differences, having envious and competitive reactions, failure to show appreciation or make apology, or accusing others of real and imagined wrongs. One woman became miffed at an acquaintance because the latter failed to speak when they passed on the street. Actually the second woman was very near-sighted, the offended woman later learned. Interpersonal antagonism cannot be always easily differentiated from substantive conflict because each subtly interacts with the other.

The discord between the Philippian women may have related to doctrine, ethics, or worship, and perhaps over some small point. Someone facetiously suggested the problem arose in the Ladies Missionary Society over whether to fold or roll the White Cross bandages. Whether or not it had a substantive basis, it flared into interpersonal conflict.

How easy for division to start over some jot or tittle, like the better word to use in liturgy. Two churches of differing denominations in a community tried to join forces to form one church. But they could not agree on whether to say, "Forgive us our debts" or "Forgive us our trespasses." So the local newspaper reported that one church went back to their trespasses while the other returned to their debts!

Two energetic Christians who do not walk close to God can push each other into Satan's service. These devout women of Philippians 4 had a disagreement, neglected to settle it loving-ly, began to avoid each other, and perhaps criticized each other to friends, spreading unhappiness all around them. Doubtless both were pained by the alienation, but neither initi-ated a reconciliation.

Paul wanted these two women to compose their differences before the issue grew to serious proportions, disrupting the fellowship, strengthening the enemy, and becoming the laughingstock of the city. How sad their differences had lasted so long. The following lines express what should have happened:

"Yes, you did too!"
"I did not!"
　　Thus the little quarrel started,
　　Thus, by unkind little words,
　　Two fond friends were parted.
"I am sorry."
"So am I."
　　Thus the little quarrel ended,
　　Thus, by loving little words,
　　Two fond hearts were mended.

Amy Carmichael, missionary to India, used a novel method to help two quarreling little girls walk in harmony. She tied their pigtails together! Since Paul couldn't use this approach, he tried another tack.

## An Urgent Plea
Each woman should have taken the initiative in going to the other to make things right. They should have met on their way to each other's house. Because of their failure, both were open to blame. Though one may have been more to blame, Paul pleads with each woman separately, first Euodias, then

Syntyche. The verb is repeated, "I beseech Euodias, and I beseech Syntyche." He handles the names alphabetically— perhaps unintentionally—like the list of credits to a TV program, or of speakers at a Bible conference. Paul shows no partiality. In the embarrassing position of seeing two beloved friends at odds, he wants to befriend both.

These names have been found over twenty times in ancient inscriptions. Euodias means "prosperous journey," or "fragrance." Syntyche means "pleasant acquaintance," or "happy chance." Someone labeled them Mrs. Fragrance and Mrs. Fortunate. Another facetiously called them Mrs. Odious and Mrs. Soon-touchy.

At any rate, Paul's appeal is strong. The root of "beseech" gives us the Comforter, a title for the third member of the Trinity (John 16:7). Paul's entreaty here echoes the Holy Spirit, coming alongside to help.

Paul exhorts these two women to "be of the same mind in the Lord" (Phil. 4:2). He had prepared them for his appeal to like-mindedness by a similar, general command in the earlier part of Philippians, "Be like-minded, having the same love, being of one accord, of one mind" (2:2). In fact, the entire second chapter of Philippians is devoted to the kind of mind every believer should have—the mind of Christ, which was one of humility. Because things equal to the same thing are equal to each other, if Euodias and Syntyche both had possessed the mind of Christ, they would have indeed been like-minded, and lowly-minded, qualities which would have soon led to reconciliation.

In his book *The Pursuit of God*, A.W. Tozer wrote: "Has it ever occurred to you that one hundred pianos all tuned to the same fork are automatically tuned to each other? They are of one accord by being tuned, not to each other, but to another standard to which each one must individually bow. So one hundred worshipers together, each one looking away to Christ, are in heart nearer to each other than they could possibly be, were they to become 'unity' conscious and turn their eyes away from God to strive for closer fellowship." Euodias and Syntyche needed to be in tune with the mind of Christ. Then they would again be in harmony with each other.

The section of Philippians that illustrates the mind of Christ (2:5-8) is the classic passage on His self-humbling. No other paragraph compasses in so short a span and with such phraseology so much truth on the condescension of the Son of God. Paul's purpose in these verses is not to provide subtle theological dogma, but to illustrate Christian duty. We ought to have the kind of mind displayed in the utter self-emptying of Christ: from the throne of God to the grave of a criminal, including from God to man (while still retaining deity), from Master to servant, from life to death (the shameful death reserved for aliens, slaves, and criminals).

As Christ stooped, so should we stoop, getting rid of pride, which is the cause of so many disputes. If Euodias and Syntyche had allowed Christ's lowly-mindedness to flood their minds, their conflict would have ended. In connection with this self-emptying passage Paul wrote: "Let nothing be done through strife or vainglory; but in lowliness of mind let each esteem other better than themselves. Look not every man on his own things, but every man also on the things of others" (2:3-4). Perhaps he had Euodias and Syntyche in mind when he so wrote.

After writing of the humility of Christ, Paul said, "Do all things without murmurings and disputings" (2:14). The two women needed to take heed. In the light of Christ's self-effacement, how small and petty were their differences! How quickly they should have put away trifling animosities and ill-will, and in the spirit of humility sought peace.

Paul's appeal "in the Lord" means as members of His body, in the consciousness of His presence, moved by His love, submitting to His guidance, strongly desiring to please Him, possessing His spirit of lowliness.

In those days letters of interest to the entire fellowship could not be copied or mimeographed for churchwide distribution. So, when Paul's letter for the Philippian congregation arrived, the church assembled, eager to hear from their beloved founder. Those present likely included Lydia and her household, the former demon-possessed girl, the jailer and his family, many other converts, and Euodias and Syntyche, doubtless not sitting side by side as perhaps they once did.

All would be listening attentively to hear Paul's words of greeting, encouragement, and edification. When the leader read, "Do all things without murmurings and disputings," both Euodias and Syntyche looked straight ahead. Then suddenly, a little later and without warning, "I beseech Euodias"—and Euodias almost jumped out of her seat. Then, "And I beseech Syntyche"—and there was a squeal from Syntyche. And they both strained to hear what came next—"that they be of the same mind in the Lord." In other words, "Patch up your quarrel! Ladies, get your act together!" What a jolt!

This public admonition via the letter probably produced embarrassment, but it was nothing like the humiliation to be suffered in the day of judgment when God will open His books to reveal the record of human deeds for which we must answer. Though the guilt of our sins has been canceled through the cross of Christ, we still have to stand before the Judgment Seat of Christ to account for works since our regeneration, either to receive reward or suffer loss (2 Cor. 5:10). Perhaps we'll be ashamed to hear our name called out in connection with a wrong done another which we have never righted. But that embarrassment is avoidable for "if we would judge ourselves, we should not be judged" (1 Cor. 11:31). Far better for these women, if they plan to sing in the choir of heaven, to practice harmony down here. Even if they patched things up, look how their names have been perpetuated through nineteen centuries of Holy Writ.

## More Help Needed

A Jewish engineer, meditating at Jerusalem's Western (Wailing) Wall, became alarmed at growing clumps of weeds hanging from the crannies of the huge stones. His training told him that the weeds could eventually tumble the wall. His warning aroused a controversy in Israel, especially when the nation's two chief rabbis, possessing equal ecclesiastical authority, took opposite views. One said that the weeds symbolize the ruin of the temple and, therefore, must not be plucked out. The other, sensing the potential damage to the wall, urged the weeds to be plucked but left near the Wall as a reminder of the Temple's destruction. When the two rabbis reached an impasse, Israel's Custodian of Holy Places was asked what he would do. His cagey answer, "Get a third opinion."

As we saw earlier, believers at odds who are unable to reconcile in a private session should call on arbiter-witnesses. Here Paul asked a "true yokefellow" to act as his third party, perhaps in full expectation that he could help calm this tempest in a teapot. Ronald Kraybill in *Repairing the Breach* says that the Apostle Paul seemed less concerned over the existence of disputes than he was over how the disputes should be settled. Kraybill points out that in this episode between ladies at Philippi, Paul does not scold because of disagreements but rather makes a direct request for the appointment of a mediator or yokefellow (p. 12).

Who was this fellow worker? Some think the word *yokefellow* here is a proper name—Synsugus, just as the women's names are specific. Others guess him to be the husband of either Euodias or Syntyche, or that Paul refers to Epaphroditus, Timothy, Silas, or even Luke, whose home was supposed to be Philippi. Whoever—it had to be a person of discretion and honor to bring together these women at variance. To heal dissension and promote Christian unity is a delicate, noble work and a needed ministry. Blessed, indeed, are the peacemakers.

If a dispute involves members of the same church, the referee should probably be a member of that fellowship too. If a problem concerns two believers from different churches, the third party should be someone with a relationship to both parties, perhaps not a member of either church. However, if a very capable arbiter should belong to either fellowship, his ability might well be utilized.

A pastor in an eastern city, realizing feuding had gone on long enough among the preachers and Christian organizations in the area, decided on a daring plan. He phoned a dozen leaders, inviting them to lunch with him in a downtown club, not telling any that the others were coming. As each man entered the private dining room, he saw another or others to whom he had not spoken for months or years. In some cases the feuds had been intense. After the blessing, the host pastor frankly told his reason for getting them together and asked if something could be done about the divisions. Before long, most were on their knees in prayer. Two who had been most bitterly at odds shook hands. Only one man said he could not ask the Lord to bless the endeavor, feeling that some present were guilty of compromise. But the rest rediscovered their oneness in Christ.

## Incentives to Reconciliation

Paul surrounds his urgent appeal for reconciliation with several low-key incentives.

• *Titles of endearment.* In the immediate verse before his plea, Paul calls the saints at Philippi, which would include the two women at odds, "my brethren." Next he speaks of them as "my joy and crown." Then he repeats, "dearly beloved." All of these terms of affection are piled up one after another in 4:1.

• *Command to stand fast.* Along with these titles of endearment in Philippians 4:1 is the command to stand fast in the Lord. This command sums up several injunctions in the previous context (3:14-21): to press on, follow Paul, live like citizens of heaven, and look for Christ's coming. These practices would make for standing in unity. When they were fighting, they were not standing fast.

• *Reminder of past teamwork.* Paul recalls the dedicated manner in which these women worked with him in the Gospel. He literally calls them fellow athletes, implying agonizing struggles midst perilous times, not only with Paul but with each other.

Then Paul thinks of other members of the team—for example, Clement and "fellow laborers whose names are in the Book of Life" (Phil. 4:3). What happy memories flood Paul's mind. He would like the team intact again. He is saying, "Get those two ladies back on the team!"

Perhaps you have fond memories of working together on some Gospel team in radio, a rescue mission, coffeehouse, or Sunday School, but now the team is broken up because of some petty difference. Why not try to resolve the disagreement and get the team going again?

These women should not be allowed to perpetuate their misbegotten misery. Paul wishes them reconciled so that they will be remembered for their devoted, meritorious service. It seems likely that the beloved apostle's plea was not in vain.

An unknown poet expresses what we hope occurred in their case:

> They walked with God in peace and love,
> But failed with one another;
> While sternly for the Faith they strove,
> Sister fell out with sister;
> But He in whom they put their trust,
> Who knew their frames that they were dust,
> Pitied and healed their weaknesses.
>
> He found them in His house of prayer,
> With one accord assembled;
> And so revealed His presence there,
> They wept with joy and trembled;
> One cup they drank, one bread they brake,
> One baptism shared, one language spake,
> Forgiving and forgiven.
>
> Then forth they went with tongues of flame
> In one blest theme uniting;
> The love of Jesus and His Name,
> God's children all uniting;

That love our theme and watchword still,
The law of love may we fulfill,
And love as we are loved.

Two women, who had not spoken to each other for two years, attended the same large church in a western city. One sat on one side, the other on the other side, both leaving after each service through separate doors to avoid contact. At one time they had been very close friends, hugging each other and verbalizing easily their love and appreciation for one another. But through a difference of opinion on a small item, they stopped speaking and began to play the game of avoiding each other. Soon time came between them. Because no attempt was made to make things right, and no communication passed between them, the small item became a large mountain.

Joanne Wallace, president of *Image Improvement*, was holding a church seminar. During the seminar she had dealt with forgiveness and new beginnings and how, as image-bearers of Jesus, we are to be verbal. One way of being verbal, she pointed out, was to tell others that we love them. During the evening session, she allowed the women to leave their seats to go to others to tell them that they are loved, or to make some wrong right. One of those two women at odds felt the Spirit of God and left her side of the church, knowing that she needed to ask forgiveness and restore the broken relationship. Then as she headed to the back of the room to find the other woman, the other woman listened to the Spirit of God. Together they wept and prayed. They also aroused their families after the seminar, and together talked till 1 A.M.

Joanne Wallace asked one of them next day if she and the other woman had agreed on the matter that had originally separated them. "No, but that doesn't matter," she responded. "We can love each other even when we don't agree, and that's what is important. We've lost two years of friendship. But now our attitudes have completely changed, and we are going back into our close, loving relationship."

Men also often need reconciliation. In 1985 a spark from a

153

few angry words started a blaze that burned throughout an association of churches in Rwanda, Africa. In 1986 at the association's annual conference many of those still hot with anger opened their hearts to the Spirit and repented. But two top leaders who had started the flame in the first place still harbored resentments. One would not go to the other's church, though he lived nearby, and avoided the other leader's house. The two spoke to each other only as absolutely necessary in the course of church business. But in April 1987 the two men publicly repented and hugged each other, the climax of a three-day spiritual life conference uniting 160 pastors in the Word and praise. Missionaries report that the breach has been completely healed. Now the two men speak to each other civilly without trying to avoid each other, just as we hope Euodias and Syntyche did back in the first century.

# 12.

# Curing the
# Boss Complex

Southern Baptist official Brooks R. Faulkner tells of a minister in an Alabama town who was about to start the monthly business meeting one Wednesday evening when a young woman about twenty-one years of age approached. "You haven't been to see me yet," she said. "After you have consulted with some of the church members you will learn that very few major decisions are made in this church without consulting me first. You didn't consult with me before bringing up this matter of an electric typewriter which you think the church office needs. I would suggest you not bother with that tonight."

The minister thought she had problems, but decided to go ahead with the business meeting agenda as planned. When the proposal for the typewriter was presented, she stood and spoke against it quite eloquently. She then made a motion that they table the proposal. The church voted against her motion. The main motion to buy the typewriter was then passed. She rose and left the business meeting.

Ten minutes later she returned with her husband towering behind her. To the minister he looked every bit of twelve feet tall. She interrupted the business meeting, saying, "Ever since I was fifteen, the pastors here have consulted with me. You are the first minister to insult me in front of my friends. You

155

should have listened to me." With that, the husband pulled out a pistol and aimed it at the minister.

By this time the deacons had surrounded the minister, while one deacon began reasoning with the young couple. Another deacon joined the caucus. After several emotional appeals, the young couple was escorted out of the church. The minister did not press charges.

From that evening on, late night phone calls and open threats occurred daily. The young woman had many relatives in the area. More than once the minister's tires were slit. After six months of harassment, the minister's wife was hospitalized from all the stress. The minister resigned without another church to go to (Broadman, 1986, pp. 36-37). Happily, most ministers do not have this kind of confrontation with "key" people who supposedly run the church.

Incidentally, the spirit of bossism is not peculiar to the church. In the world of business, executives are often jockeying for top spot in the organization. The ploy for power is common even in family businesses. Sons of Bosses is an organization of young men who have taken over control of family companies or are in line for the top job because of heredity. Such men seem to have special problems. Often their fathers are intensely competitive, viewing successor-sons as threats or embarrassments, not welcome associates. Some fathers want to keep running the show even when their sons have become better qualified. Yet some sons want supreme authority before they are capable of exercising it. One son, unwilling to wait for the day his father would yield power, suggested his dad take a vacation in Europe, then seized control in his absence. The truth is that human nature—whether paternal or filial—relishes control over people.

This spirit often invades the church. First-century Diotrophes was such a man. The Apostle John wrote a congregation these words about this officious character in their midst: "I wrote unto the church, but Diotrophes, who loveth to have the preeminence among them, receiveth us not. Wherefore, if I come, I will remember his deeds which he doeth, prating against us with malicious words; and not content therewith, neither doth he himself receive the brethren, and forbiddeth them that would, and casteth them out of the church" (3 John 9-10).

Joe, a modern Diotrophes, who owns his own company, and before whose sole authority all ten employees bow in complete dependence for their jobs, carries this autocratic spirit over to the official church board where, unable to stand opposition, he has to have his way or else. In business no one dares block him, but in the church board meetings he is frequently challenged and even outvoted, causing him to seethe and embarrass fellow board members with his resentful remarks. Some have resigned the board and even left the church because of his dictatorial methods.

## Leader versus Boss

Management experts describe the various styles of leadership as *bureaucratic*—operating by rule and regulations; *laissez-faire*—permissive; *participative*—others sharing in decisions; and *dictatorial*—one-man rule. No question about Diotrophes' mode—he was an iron-fisted autocrat.

We must distinguish between bossism and leadership. Every church needs leaders with the gift of government who have vision, set goals, implement these objectives, and see them through to completion—perhaps stirring up a few waves in the process. But this isn't bossism. Leaders who share authority accept an occasional negative vote, but a boss demands his way regardless of opposition. Diotrophes not only told everyone else what to do, but took strong measures against any who stood in his way. This, in turn, required drastic action according to the Apostle John. Here's what Diotrophes had done.

● *Diotrophes rejected the traveling preachers of whom John had written.* A letter John had written this church about some itinerant preachers had fallen into the hand of Diotrophes, likely because he was an officer. Magnifying his authority, he haughtily refused to receive these travelers, an insult to the apostle whom they represented. John then wrote the well-loved Gaius, whose godly walk and generous hospitality were well known, to ask him to welcome these visitors.

- *Diotrophes prated maliciously against John and others.* Prating, occurring only here in the New Testament, carries the idea of boiling up hollow bubbles. A related word is translated "tattlers" (1 Tim. 5:13). His pretentious words characterized him as a wicked windbag.

- *Diotrophes forbade others to receive the itinerant preachers. Diotrophes put out of the church those that wanted to welcome the itinerant preachers.* Somehow succeeding in getting the majority under his thumb, he pushed himself forward to usurp the leadership of the church, then ousting any who opposed him.

How often in history the man with top authority has resented the presence of even a loyal second-in-command. Richard Wolff in *Man at the Top* asks: "Is this what happened to the French Premier Pompidou in May 1968? Was he fired by General DeGaulle because the Premier had become too popular? Pompidou kept the government running during the May riots in 1968. Pompidou masterminded the campaign which brought DeGaulle back into power. His reward was to be dismissed. His success became a threat to DeGaulle. Willful and arbitrary, DeGaulle acted in true autocratic fashion, retaining a firm grip on the levers of power" (Tyndale, 1969, pp. 108-109).

More than one church officer has thwarted attempts to place on a board or committee a person whose achievements and talents might endanger that officer's supremacy. Even pastors have arranged for the departure of assistants whose ability and popularity became a threat to their own eminence. The love of power is not far behind love of money in subverting character.

Diotrophes is described as one "who loveth to have the preeminence." In the original language, preeminence is a compound word meaning "to love to be first." This compound is found only here in the New Testament. The second word of the compound, *to be first*, is used in Colossians 1:18, referring to Christ: "that in all things He might have the preeminence." Diotrophes was guilty of dangerous presumption.

Diotrophes was the archetype of vain, self-seeking, self-elected overseers who are obsessed with lording it over their brethren and browbeating all who get in their way. He was the forerunner of the "church boss," a type known wherever the church has gone.

Lyle E. Schaller in *The Change Agent* (Abingdon, 1972) deals with the topic of power in the local church. Power may reside in many persons, including not only the minister and the elected leaders, but also in others who do not appear to be power figures, but who do have tremendous collective power. Two-thirds of a congregation, disapproving of some action taken by the leadership, can apply sanctions to reverse the decision, such as withholding offerings, staying away from church, or even joining another church. But often the reins of power reside in one person.

A pastor in Iowa told of a case involving a man in his congregation who took him aside and gave him $100 every month. Another man offered to buy him a new suit every year. Though not refusing at first, he began to realize both donors had ulterior, political motives in mind. Not wishing to be owned by either of these men, he determined to decline their gifts henceforth.

A rural pastor was befriended by an older deacon who generously shared his garden produce and insisted on keeping the young pastor's beat-up Ford filled with gas from the tank behind the barn. One day the deacon asked a favor of the pastor which went against the pastor's conscience. When he refused, the deacon told him to look for another church. Since this deacon also gave over 30 percent of the church's total budget, the pastor found that his ministry was finished.

In a small western church, the owner of a company contributed over half the church's income. Going for his first haircut, the pastor thought the barber was joking when he said, "Oh, you're at the church Mr. X owns." Before long the pastor discovered it was no joke. Mr. X phoned at 9 and 11:30 each morning to make sure the pastor was keeping regular office hours.

A seminary professor asked his pastoral theology class to draw a chart of the lines of authority in their home churches. The students drew nice boxes with lines running clearly from one to another. Then he asked them to draw a diagram with the actual decision-making process. One student formed a circle of small circles with spokes connected to a well-defined circle in the middle. This circle represented the man who ran the church and was marked "Ralph." The small circles represented the congregation.

Greek scholar A.T. Robertson, in an article on Diotrophes for a church magazine, portrayed him as one who wants to control a church according to his own whims. Subsequently twenty deacons from various parts of the country wrote the editor to cancel their subscriptions because of this "personal attack" made on them!

A church boss complex may develop in a man who has been passed over for promotion at work, so he kicks up a fuss at church. Or a man who is dominated by his wife at home may try to rule in his church.

Often a power struggle comes to the fore when the church begins to grow. The influx of new people is resented by the old-timers because they sense a potential loss of power. This struggle has been called the "pioneer-homesteader" conflict.

Another power struggle evolves when an individual is completely wrapped up in his own particular ministry, unable to see any other service than the one in which he is interested. So, the church must revolve around his "thing." A *Leadership* article called this "the subtle sin of ergocentricity." "Ergo" comes from the word for "work." Everything centers around one's work or ministry.

● *Strong-minded but lowly-minded.* A pastor is not to be a tyrant or lord it over his sheep (1 Peter 5:2-3). Political leaders typically exercise ironclad authority over the citizens. A pastor should be authoritative without being authoritarian.

A person can be strong-minded and still have the mind of

Christ. He can suggest ideas, take initiative, research facts, and make a strong presentation. But if his idea is voted down, he will be a good loser, bowing to the majority. He will not sulk or make waves.

Since members in general try to be nice, they sometimes give in to hard-nosed fellow members. To avoid argument or an unpleasant public scene, they give a belligerent minority the leeway by default to undercut the pastor and veto programs. But a healthy congregation should never permit one person, or a couple of families, or a group of any magnitude to run the church. Without declaring open warfare, healthy members should be nice but firm.

How should a church boss be handled? The directions in an earlier chapter dealing with brothers-at-odds should be followed. A person offended by the overbearing bossism of a church leader should schedule a private appointment to face the dominating personality with evidence of his oppressive conduct. If the attempt makes no dent on the self-styled boss, then the person offended must seek additional witnesses who agree on the need for change in leadership style. If a second confrontation produces no remorse on the part of this modern Diotrophes, the matter should be taken to the congregation. At this point the church will have to choose the kind of leadership it wants. Drastic action may be required, at least removing him from his place of leadership, if not excommunicating him on the grounds of divisive conduct. The aged John, with a trace of youthful thunder in his writing, threatened, "Wherefore, if I come, I will remember his deeds." John would confront Diotrophes before all.

## The Boss Within

Though a Diotrophes should be dealt with swiftly and firmly, a more pressing problem in most churches is how to overcome the spirit of bossism in our own hearts. We need to counteract the chief syndrome that dissipates our energy in recognition-seeking rather than in getting God's work done.

One firm has made headlines out of deflating a person's ego.

# When the Saints Come Storming In

It signs contracts to provide a pie and have it thrown by one of its employees into the face of a pompous victim or thick-skinned friend. In its first few months over sixty hits were made on disbelieving victims at a minimum of $35 per splash. Imagine the surprise of a dignified executive waiting for an elevator when a stranger whips a pie out of a cardboard box and mashes it into his astonished face, giving the pie a professional twist at impact, sending the goo meandering down his face and dropping off the chin onto his immaculate shirt and tie! A member of the company said, "A pie in the face brings a man's dignity down to where it should be, and puts the big guys on the same level with everyone else." But a more likely result is a raging court suit or repayment in kind!

The New Testament suggests several helps for overcoming Diotrophes-like self-centeredness—and with God's help all things are possible!

● *Consider others as worthy of greater honor.* Delicate situations arise in churches when we feel we aren't getting our rightful position, privilege, or prestige. Some less-deserving person is given a prominent seat on the platform; someone is not asked to do a job for which he thinks he has the ability; someone else is asked to serve on a choice committee; or our service is not noticed and commended. The New Testament reply is, "In honor preferring one another" (Rom. 12:10). And, "In lowliness of mind let each esteem other better than themselves" (Phil. 2:3). If each of us deems himself as a nobody, and then someone takes him for a somebody, the result will be pure profit.

Jesus counseled His followers not to claim honor by choosing top spots at a dinner. Deliberately building a big ecclesiastical empire, or seeking the limelight, or accepting an important position because it is strategic and influential betrays a Diotrophes mentality. Theologian Francis Schaeffer has said we should consciously take the lowest place unless the Lord Himself forces us into a more responsible one. Otherwise we may find ourselves "over our depth" with ensuing difficulties that cause unrest of soul and decrease of spiritual power, and certainly discovering that whoever exalts self will be abased.

Schaeffer also pointed out in *No Little People* that there are no "big people" and no "little people" in God's sight, just dedicated and undedicated people. The seemingly little is big if that is where God wants us. Two little girls built a shack for a clubhouse in their backyard, then scribbled on the wall these perceptive rules: (1) Nobody act big. (2) Nobody act small. (3) Everybody act medium.

German author Goethe and composer Beethoven were out walking. Wherever they went people pointed them out, and Goethe exclaimed, "Isn't it maddening? I simply cannot escape this homage!" Beethoven replied, "Don't be too much distressed by it. It's just possible that some of it may be for me."

How different from the attitude of Principal Cairns, headmaster of an English school. As a member of a group assigned to sit at the front of a great gathering, he walked onto the platform in a line with the other dignitaries. His appearance was met by a burst of applause. Cairns stepped back to let the man behind pass him, then began to applaud his colleague. In his modesty he assumed the applause was for another. He may have a prominent place at Jesus' table.

● *Submit one to another.* Submission is one manifestation of being filled with the Holy Spirit (Eph. 5:18-21). Under the wrong kind of spirits men become self-assertive. Under the Holy Spirit, they become humble, not heady.

John Owen, one-time chancellor of Oxford University, used to go to hear the unschooled John Bunyan preach when the tinker came to London. King Charles II expressed surprise that so learned a person would listen to so uneducated a man as Bunyan. Owen replied, "Had I the tinker's abilities, please your Majesty, I should gladly relinquish my learning."

Submission is voluntary accommodation to another, displaying modesty, humility, unwillingness to unnecessarily dispute, gentleness, forbearance, contentment. Such an attitude reduces the friction of human interaction and contributes greatly to a church's peace and unity. No one, including pastors, should be exempt from accountability to some other person, board, or committee. Each committee member should submit his ideas to the judgment of the rest of his committee peers. Where there is submission on both sides of an issue, there is not debasement, but union. In an era of independent action, how needed is a reminder of the importance of mutual subordination.

A newspaper item captioned "The Principle of the Thing" told how stubbornness had caused a split in Japan's Stubbornness Club, formed a year earlier by twenty people who considered themselves obstinate but who wanted to be constructive members of society. Their monthly meetings became so clamorous that the vice-president resigned to form a rival but more discreet Society for the Preservation of Stubbornness.

Too often church splits are caused by stubborn Christians who hold tenaciously to their own opinions, often in secondary matters. Though claiming to hold to "the principles" of the issue, they are more likely defending their own prestige and personal views, unwilling to submit to one another lovingly.

When a driver came to a narrow bridge, he noticed a sign, "Yield." He thought he remembered a similar sign on the other side of the bridge when he drove in the other direction earlier that day. Sure enough, after making sure no traffic was coming, on crossing the bridge he verified the fact that signs had been posted on both sides of the bridge. Asking drivers from both directions to give the right of way to the other was a logical and courteous way of avoiding head-on collisions. Likewise, the biblical command to be subject to one another is a rational and benevolent device to prevent interpersonal clashing.

Both college youth and a women's group wanted to reserve the kitchen and fellowship hall for their Christmas parties on the same night. Both felt entitled to the facilities, the college youth because many of their members were home only over the Christmas holiday, and the women because they were a longtime established organization. Before the incident could

flare into serious conflict, wiser hearts in both groups pre-
vailed. Each organization offered to select another date, the
women finally moving their party to another night which, in the
long run, fortuitously turned out to their advantage.

● *Serve one another.* At the annual homecomings of William and Mary College in Virginia, a number of prominent
people, including a college president, a governor, and well-
known business and professional leaders are seen wearing
white jackets. The jackets signify that these men earned all or
much of their way through college by waiting on tables. The
New Testament asks all believers to join the "Christian Order
of the White Jackets" when it urges, "By love serve one another" (Gal. 5:13).

Jesus' disciples displayed the Diotrophes syndrome on at
least three occasions by arguing about which of them would
have top spot in His coming kingdom. The first time, Jesus'
response was to place a child before them and exhort the
disciples to childlike humility (Mark 9:33-37).

On the second occasion, Jesus pointed out that secular leaders sought the number one position in order to wield power
and manipulate people tyrannically, but in Christ's circle the
leader needs the opposite motive. "Whosoever will be great
among you, shall be your minister: and whosoever of you will
be the chiefest, shall be servant of all." Then to contrast the
selfish aspirations of His disciples, Jesus gave the example of
His own service, pointing out that "even the Son of man came
not to be ministered unto, but to minister, and to give His life
a ransom for many" (Mark 10:43-45).

The third instance occurred in the Upper Room with the
Saviour's death less than twenty-four hours away. The disciples were debating who should rank the highest in the coming
kingdom when they should have been competing to see who
would be first in washing each other's feet. Though basin and
towel had been provided, no aspiring leader would abdicate his
throne of hoped-for preeminence to kneel before his subjects.
As they looked away from towel and basin with studied indifference, the amazing happened: Jesus rose to give a graphic

demonstration that should have forever dulled their lust for leadership. The Lord of Glory, at whose beck legions of angels would immediately respond, chose the servant's place and took the soiled feet of the disciples in His own hands. "If I then, your Lord and Master, have washed your feet; ye also ought to wash one another's feet" (John 13:14). His action told His followers to seek service, not sovereignty. He made forever noble the Order of the White Jackets.

The son of a wealthy family in the Philippines enrolled in the Bible Institute of Manilla. On his arrival he was greeted by an unimpressive man in shirt sleeves who graciously carried the wealthy son's suitcase to his assigned room. Before the coatless man left, the rich lad quickly inspected the room and complained of the dirt in the bathroom. A few minutes later the same man, soiled and sweaty, emerged from the bathroom with scrub brush and pail in hand. That evening, at opening convocation, that boy was stunned to learn that this unimpressive man who had so uncomplainingly performed those menial tasks was none other than the president of the Bible institute.

Interestingly, all three recorded disputes among the disciples as to who should be greatest occurred right after Jesus had spoken of His coming death and future kingdom glory. Somehow their thoughts slid past the cross to dwell on the kingdom splendor, making them ask for positions of honor in that glorious, coming realm.

But even for us, who have a nineteen-century vantage point, how quickly after private devotions or communion service or public preaching do our minds divert from the supreme sacrifice of Christ to our own importance, our rights, our dignity, our position, our authority! When tempted to thoughts of preeminence and to having our own way in the church, we need to turn to Calvary to behold the Servant of servants whose whole life was one continuous ministry, not of bossing, and who finally gave His very lifeblood in one supreme sacrifice for others. Earnest meditation on the Cross of Jesus should quell our desire for domination, and help put a stop to the unholy wars within the church.

## Curing the Boss Complex

When I survey the wondrous cross
On which the Prince of Glory died,
My richest gain I count but loss,
And pour contempt on all my pride.
                              —Isaac Watts